Act of Justice

ACT OF JUSTICE

Lincoln's
Emancipation
Proclamation
and the
Law of War

Burrus M. Carnahan

THE UNIVERSITY PRESS OF KENTUCKY

Publication of this volume was made possible in part by a grant
from the National Endowment for the Humanities.

Editorial and Sales Offices: The University Press of Kentucky
663 South Limestone Street, Lexington, Kentucky 40508-4008
www.kentuckypress.com

11 10 09 08 07   5 4 3 2 1

Library of Congress Cataloging-in-Publication Data

Carnahan, Burrus M., 1944–
  Act of justice : Lincoln's Emancipation Proclamation and the law of war / Burrus M.
Carnahan.
    p. cm.
  Includes bibliographical references and index.
  ISBN 978-0-8131-2463-6 (hardcover : alk. paper) 1. United States. President
(1861–1865 : Lincoln). Emancipation Proclamation. 2. Slaves—Emancipation—
United States. 3. African Americans—Legal status, laws, etc.—History—19th
century. 4. Lincoln, Abraham, 1809–1865—Political and social views. 5. Military
law—United States—History—19th century. 6. Executive power—United States—
History—19th century. 7. Constitutional history—United States. I. Title.
  E453.C375 2007
  973.7'14—dc22   2007017936

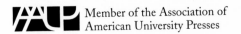

To Cindy, for her support and encouragement

Contents

Acknowledgments

Many have generously given their time to review the manuscript for this book and offer corrections and suggestions. I especially thank George Anastaplo, Harold Holzer, Edward Steers, and Frank Williams for their valuable help. Of course, these eminent scholars are not responsible for any errors remaining in the text. Those are my responsibility alone.

Parts of chapters 1, 5, and 9 were previously published by Lincoln Memorial University of Harrogate, Tennessee, in the spring 2001 and spring 2006 issues of the *Lincoln Herald* (volume 103, number 1, and volume 108, number 1, respectively).

Introduction

Scarcely any political question arises in the United States that is not resolved, sooner or later, into a judicial question.

—Alexis de Tocqueville, *Democracy in America*,
Book I, Chapter 16

Only once did Abraham Lincoln explain to the American people the legal principles underpinning his Emancipation Proclamation. On August 26, 1863, Lincoln sent James C. Conkling a wide-ranging defense of the proclamation on political, practical, and military grounds that was intended to be read to a mass meeting in Springfield, Illinois. In one key paragraph, President Lincoln answered critics who argued that the proclamation infringed on the constitutional protection of private property. "I think," he began, "the constitution invests its commander-in-chief with the law of war in time of war." The most that his critics could say, "if so much," was that "slaves are property." "Is there," he continued,

> has there ever been—any question that by the law of war, property, both of enemies and friends, may be taken when needed? And is it not needed whenever taking it, helps us, or hurts the enemy? Armies, the world over, destroy enemies' property when they can not use it; and even destroy their own to keep it from the enemy. Civilized belligerents do all in their power to help themselves, or hurt the enemy, except a few things regarded as barbarous or cruel. Among the exceptions are the massacre of vanquished foes, and non-combatants, male and female.[1]

What was the president trying to communicate when he invoked the "law of war," and what reason did he have to believe this would satisfy the critics, or at least some of them? What events led him to use this justification for the proclamation, and what were the legal and policy implications of this choice? This work is an attempt to answer these questions.

Although there have been many thoughtful efforts to explore the constitutional context of the Emancipation Proclamation, the rest of the proclamation's legal context remains largely uncharted territory. Another purpose of this work is to set out this legal context. For most of his life, Abraham Lincoln earned his living by practicing law. He was a general practitioner, whose work ranged from the defense of accused criminals to the defense of property rights. When, as president, Lincoln weighed the issues raised by his most important and controversial exercise of the war powers, the Emancipation Proclamation, he would necessarily have viewed these in light of his practical knowledge of American law.

The legal context for Lincoln's decisions differed significantly from that of more recent presidential actions. Today, for example, citizens who want to challenge the constitutionality of a government act typically apply to a Federal court for an injunction, or court order, to prevent Federal officials from carrying out the challenged action. In the nineteenth century, however, injunctions were much less freely used. Both state and Federal courts were reluctant to issue injunctions unless it could clearly be shown that a later suit for money damages would be an inadequate remedy. In Lincoln's era, the principal way to challenge the legality of an official act was to sue individual government officers for money damages. This practice, which the United States had inherited from the English common law, meant that if the courts rejected the Emancipation Proclamation, every U.S. Army officer who sheltered a refugee from slavery would be liable to pay aggrieved slave owners the value of their lost property.

The consequences of Lincoln's decision to rely on the law of war as a source of executive power are still with us. All war presidents since his time have invoked the international law of war as a measure and source of their powers as commander in chief of the armed forces. The use of that power has often been controversial. Most recently, following the invasion of Afghanistan, the United States has claimed the right under the law of war to hold enemy combatants indefinitely without criminal charges. Although a deeply divided Supreme Court affirmed this power in 2004 (in the case of *Hamdi v. Rumsfeld*), the continued detention of these men at the Guantanamo Naval Base in Cuba has given rise to vehement criticism, especially in Europe. It is perhaps ironic that the same legal theory invoked to deprive hundreds of Guantanamo prisoners of their liberty was used by President Lincoln to free thousands of enslaved Americans.

1

Planting the Seed: Charles Sumner and John Quincy Adams

Senator Charles Sumner of Massachusetts hurried to the White House as soon as he learned that the Confederates had fired on Fort Sumter in April 1861. There he urged President Lincoln to use his power as commander in chief of the armed forces under the Constitution to free the slaves in the rebellious states. As commander in chief he could, Sumner argued, use any means necessary to suppress the rebellion. Those means included a proclamation offering freedom to the enemy's slaves.[1]

Sumner's advice must have been startling to the new president. Lincoln's law practice in Illinois had not prepared him to deal with questions arising under the international law of war.[2] Barely a month earlier, Lincoln had publicly reaffirmed in his Inaugural Address that he had "no purpose, directly or indirectly to interfere with the institutions of slavery in the States where it exists," and that he believed he had no legal right to do so.[3] In 1861, most American lawyers would have agreed with Lincoln that the Federal government had no constitutional power to alter or abolish slavery in the states where it already existed.[4]

At about the same time, an old friend and political ally of Lincoln's from Illinois also started to urge the necessity of emancipation. Three years older than Lincoln, Orville Hickman Browning regarded himself as the president's superior in both breeding and intelligence. An enthusiastic, if conservative, Republican activist, he had undertaken the task of keeping the president up-to-date on the political climate in his home state, as well as that of offering national policy advice to his supposedly unsophisticated friend.

Browning first hesitantly predicted that the war would have an impact on slavery at the end of a letter dated April 18. After reassuring the new president that "you are adequate to the emergency; [and] that you will meet it as it should be met," he reported on the state of "public sentiment" in his region; then, in the closing paragraph, he made his prediction: "I think I have a clear perception of the ultimate destiny of the Cotton States. They have invited their doom. They can never be again what they have once been. God is entering into judgment with them. He is dealing with them, and will deal with the colored race there also."[5] In a letter drafted at the end of April, Browning spelled out the implications of his prophesy for the Lincoln administration. "The time is not yet, but it will come when it will be necessary for you to march an army into the South, and proclaim freedom to the slaves. When it does come, do it. Dont [sic] hesitate. You are fighting for national life—for your own individual life. God has raised you up for a great work. Go boldly forward in the course his providence points you. Do not look back—do not falter, or he may forsake you."[6]

Browning and Lincoln were both lawyers and had practiced before the same courts in Illinois. It is therefore curious that, unlike Senator Sumner, Browning did not tell his friend what legal authority he thought the president had to proclaim freedom for the slaves. Browning would address this deficiency later in the year.

Unlike Orville Browning, Senator Charles Sumner had already formed definite ideas about the president's legal authority to free slaves as commander in chief of the army and navy. These the senator had absorbed from his political mentor, former president, and longtime congressman John Quincy Adams. Adams, in turn, had become familiar with the link between war and emancipation while serving as secretary of state for President James Monroe. At that time, one of the primary diplomatic issues facing the United States was the assertion of American claims for slaves freed by the British Royal Navy during the War of 1812. Most such claims arose from the operations of Royal Navy warships deployed in Chesapeake Bay in 1814 under the command of Admiral George Cockburn.

The admiralty's orders to Cockburn included explicit instructions on dealing with American slaves. Without inciting a slave insurrection, British forces operating in American waters were to offer sanctuary to refugees from slavery and were authorized to promise them freedom if they defected. British forces were specifically ordered not to forcibly return any refugee to slavery. They were, however, to try to persuade them to join His Majesty's armed forces. Men who did not enlist were to be taken to British colonies for resettlement, along with women, children, and those otherwise unsuited to military service. On April 2, 1814, Admiral Cockburn issued a proclamation reflecting these orders, and by September he had organized 300 escaped slaves into a unit of "Royal Colonial Marines" serving in the Chesapeake. By the end of the war, 3,600 slaves had fled to the British.[7]

Despite the admiralty's order not to return fleeing slaves to their American owners, the Treaty of Ghent, which ended the War of 1812, appeared to obligate the government of Great Britain to do just that (or so it could be interpreted). By the winter of 1814–1815, both the British and the American negotiators were eager to end the war as quickly as possible, and their haste is evident in the convoluted wording of several provisions in the treaty. For example, article 1, dealing with captured government and private property, stated that: "All territory, places, and possessions whatsoever taken by either party from the other during the war, . . . shall be restored without delay, and without causing any destruction or carrying away any of the artillery or other public property originally captured in the said forts or places, . . . or any slaves or other private property."[8]

To his credit, Captain John Lavelle, the British officer in command on the scene, refused to comply with American demands for the return of refugee slaves, and his superiors in the Royal Navy backed him up. Captain Lavelle and Admiral Cockburn interpreted the Treaty of Ghent to require the return only of slaves originally in captured forts or other places, and not those who had fled to the British in accordance with Admiral Cockburn's proclamation. The refugees were eventually sent to live as free persons in Canada, Bermuda, and the Bahamas, and the resulting dispute between the United States and England introduced Secretary of State John Quincy Adams to the practice of military emancipation.

After protracted negotiations, the two countries agreed to submit the dispute to arbitration by the czar of Russia, who on April 22, 1818, decided that under the terms of the treaty the United States was entitled to compensation for the slaves "carried away" by British forces. At one point during these proceedings, Secretary of State Adams instructed the American minister in St. Petersburg to deny that the British had any general legal right under international law to emancipate the slaves of an enemy in war. Since Adams argued later in his career that such a right did exist, he has been criticized for inconsistency.[9] This criticism ignores Adams's duty as secretary of state to formulate the best arguments he could to support the claims of slave-owning American citizens, regardless of his personal views on the international law of military emancipation.

John Quincy Adams succeeded James Monroe as president in 1824. After being defeated for reelection, he ran for the U.S. House of Representatives, where he served as a member of the Massachusetts delegation for more than a decade. There, from 1836 to 1844, Adams waged a personal crusade against a gag rule that prevented the Congress from even considering constituent petitions opposed to slavery. Before 1836, Adams had expressed little concern about the morality of American slavery, and his opposition to the gag rule was initially based on his view that it directly violated the right of petition guaranteed by the First Amendment. The struggle against the gag rule slowly drew him into the antislavery cause.[10]

Congressman Adams's first observations on slavery and the war power did not explicitly assert a military power to emancipate slaves. Rather, he laid the conceptual foundations for such an assertion. On May 18, 1836, a House committee reported three proposed resolutions that would establish the ban on antislavery petitions. The first resolution stated the purported legal basis for the gag: "*Resolved,* That Congress possesses no constitutional authority to interfere in any way with the institution of slavery in any of the States of this Confederacy [i.e., the United States]." When called upon to vote, Adams announced his intention to argue that the resolution was "false and utterly untrue." Other congressmen immediately objected that debate was out of order at this point in the proceedings; members were to vote yea or nay, and that was all. Adams sat down, but he would not remain silent for long.[11]

His chance to return to the issue came on May 26, when the House debated a resolution to authorize relief measures for refugees from the Seminole Indian war. A significant fraction of the hostile Seminoles were of African descent—escaped slaves who had adopted the culture of their Native American hosts. This gave Adams an opening to state his opinions on slavery and the war power.

Sir, in the authority given to Congress by the Constitution of the United States to declare war, all the powers incidental to

war are, by necessary implication, conferred upon the government of the United States. Now, the powers incidental to war
are derived, not from their internal municipal source [i.e., the
Constitution], but from the laws and usages of nations. . . . The
war power is limited only by the laws and usages of nations.
This power is tremendous; it is strictly constitutional, but it
breaks down every barrier so anxiously erected for the protection of liberty, of property, and of life. This, sir, is the power
which authorizes you to pass the resolution now before you,
and no other.[12]

This opinion was also behind his opposition to the earlier resolution
declaring that Congress had no authority to interfere with slavery "in
any way." The Federal response to a slave rebellion, for example, would
clearly empower the U.S. government to interfere with slavery in the
states.

Suppose the case of a servile war, complicated, as to some extent it is even now, with an Indian war; suppose Congress were
called to raise armies, to supply money from the whole Union
to suppress a servile insurrection: would they have no authority to interfere with the institution of slavery? The issue of a
servile war may be disastrous; it may become necessary for the
master of the slave to recognize his emancipation by a treaty
of peace: can it for an instant be pretended that Congress, in
such a contingency, would have no authority to interfere with
the institution of slavery, in any way? Why it would be equivalent to saying that Congress have no constitutional authority to
make peace. . . . From the instant that your slaveholding states
become the theatre of a war, civil, servile, or foreign war, from
that instant the war powers of Congress extend to interference
with the institution of slavery, in every way by which it can be
interfered with.[13]

To the slave states, Adams's most startling assertion was that the Federal
war power was not limited by the Constitution but only the law of nations, or international law. Without specifically mentioning slavery, the
text of the Constitution accommodated it thorough such devices as the
fugitive slave clause and the grant to slave states of extra representation

in the House for three-fifths of their unfree populations; the South relied on the Constitution as the bulwark holding back abolitionist efforts to attack the peculiar institution through the Federal government.

The constitutional reasoning behind Adams's position was first set out by U.S. Supreme Court justice Joseph Story. In an 1814 judicial opinion arising out of the War of 1812, Story declared of the president that "he must, as an incident of the office, have a right to employ all the usual and customary means acknowledged in war, to carry it [i.e., a declaration of war] into effect." Furthermore, this "power to carry war into effect gives every incidental power which the law of nations authorizes and approves in a state of war."[14] Justice Story later expanded this reasoning to include congressional war powers in his book *Commentaries on the Constitution of the United States.* According to the commentaries, the power to declare war "includes the exercise of all the ordinary rights of belligerents; and Congress may therefore pass suitable laws to enforce them. They may authorize the seizure and condemnation of the property of the enemy within, or without the territory of the United States; and the confiscation of debts due to the enemy."[15] By this reasoning, when the Constitution granted Congress and the president (as commander in chief of the army, navy, and militia) the power to make war, it must be assumed that the Founders wanted the United States to win its wars. Therefore, the Constitution must have also granted the Federal government all the legitimate powers any potential enemy nation would have had—"all the ordinary rights of belligerents." What those war-winning rights were could be determined by looking at the crystallized experiences and practices of other war-making governments—the "law of nations."

According to a standard twentieth-century textbook, "the Law of Nations, or International Law, may be defined as the body of rules and principles of action which are binding upon civilized states in their relations with one another." These rules and principles are derived from treaties and international custom, the latter in the sense of "a usage felt by those who follow it to be an obligatory one."[16] Historically, the doctrine of "natural law"—that is, rules of law derived from the application of human reason to the problem of how nations should behave—has also had an important impact on the law of nations.

To our postmodern age, appeals to the law of nations and the law of nature may appear naïve and even cynical. In the political world of the early American Republic, however, these concepts were taken quite seriously. The Declaration of Independence itself had appealed to "unalienable rights" created by the laws of nature to justify the American Revolution. The need for a federal government powerful enough to enforce American obligations under the law of nations was one of the major motivations behind the drafting and adoption of the Constitution in 1787.

For example, in 1784, the Continental Congress set out to establish commercial and diplomatic relations with the kingdoms and republics of Europe. Congress approved a model treaty of commerce and friendship to be used as the basis of negotiations, and sent Thomas Jefferson to join Benjamin Franklin and John Adams in France. These three diplomats were to negotiate treaties of friendship and commerce with as many governments as possible. After two years, it was clear that their mission had failed. Only one treaty, with Frederick the Great of Prussia, had been concluded. Austria, Denmark, Sardinia, the Papal States, Tuscany, Saxony, and Russia expressed no interest in treaty relations with the new republic. The inability of the United States to enforce its treaty obligations under the Articles of Confederation had become so notorious that European powers saw little advantage in concluding agreements with it.

State governments, including their courts, often failed to comply with the terms of the 1783 Treaty of Paris, which required compensation for British property confiscated by the states during the Revolution. In retaliation, the British government refused to evacuate its military garrisons on U.S. territory north of the Ohio River, and there was little Congress could do in response. Neither could Congress prevent Virginia from granting safe haven to a pirate wanted by France, America's most crucial ally in the Revolution.[17] When the secretary of the French Legation in Philadelphia was assaulted in violation of the law of nations, Congress had to rely on the Pennsylvania authorities to punish the perpetrator in the absence of a federal judiciary.[18]

To gain respect among the European nations in the 1780s, and to prevent irresponsible state governments from plunging the entire country into war, the United States had to create a central government with sufficient power to enforce its obligations under the law of nations. As much as any other defect in the Articles of Confederation, this need led directly to the adoption of the Constitution of 1787, which declared treaties to be the "supreme Law of the Land," enforceable in the new Federal courts, and authorized Congress to "regulate Commerce with foreign Nations" and punish "Offenses against the Law of Nations." When John Quincy Adams referred to the law of nations in 1836, he was invoking one of the core values at the foundation of the Constitution.

Adams was remarkably prescient in speculating that the Second Seminole War would involve the Federal government with slavery. However, he failed to foresee that this would come through the action of the U.S. Army, not of Congress. One historian called the Second Seminole War "the most difficult and costly of any the United States has ever waged against any of its Native American tribes."[19] The Seminoles had long provided sanctuary to escaped slaves from Florida and Georgia, adopting them into their society and culture. The white population of the region insisted that, in accordance with Federal Indian policy, the Seminoles be deported west of the Mississippi. Many Seminole bands refused to move. Hostilities began on December 28, 1835, when the Seminoles attacked and annihilated more than 100 U.S. soldiers who were on a march from Tampa to Ocala. The Seminoles killed all the soldiers but three (who survived by feigning death), and captured their guide, a slave named Luis Pacheco, who later changed sides and joined the Seminoles.[20]

Florida soon became the graveyard of American military reputations. In January 1836, command of U.S. forces was given to Major General Winfield Scott, a hero of the War of 1812 (and later of the war with Mexico). He was relieved in July and ordered to Washington to face a Court of Inquiry on the failure of his campaign.[21] By November 1836, Scott's successor, Florida territorial governor Richard Call, had also been relieved of command. In December he was replaced by Major General Thomas Jesup, recently successful in a campaign against the Creek tribe in Georgia.

The War Department granted General Jesup the dubious privilege of remaining in command long enough to learn some hard lessons. One of the most important was that the African Americans living with the Seminoles, whether newly escaped slaves or established tribal members, were highly influential opponents of submission to the government. If the Seminoles surrendered, these African Americans faced return to slavery, not merely removal to new lands west of the Mississippi.

After a successful military campaign in 1837, General Jesup convinced several Seminole leaders to surrender their bands and accept transportation to the Indian Territory. He also persuaded a few of these leaders to secretly round up and turn over the escaped slaves among them. When this arrangement was revealed to the other tribal leaders, the peace agreement collapsed, the Seminoles in army custody escaped, and the war resumed. "The negroes rule the Indians," Jesup concluded, "and it is important that they should feel themselves secure; if they should become alarmed and hold out, the war will be renewed."[22]

In March 1838, Jesup tried another tactic to placate the black Seminoles, and issued an order that any of them "who separated themselves from the Indians and delivered themselves up to the Commanding officer of the Troops, should be free."[23] Jesup was relieved of command in May, but his successor, General Zachary Taylor, retained his emancipation policy. By early June, Taylor had collected more than 300 Seminoles at Tampa for transportation to the Indian Territory. Many were claimed as escaped slaves by their purported owners, both in Florida and later in New Orleans, but General Taylor and his superior, General Edmund P. Gaines, refused to surrender them on the grounds that they were prisoners of war. By the end of the war, the army had sent an estimated 400 to 500 African Americans to the West and freedom, including Luis Pacheco, the guide captured in the initial battle. Some slave owners appealed to Congress for compensation, but without result.[24] Just as John Quincy Adams had suggested at the beginning of the Seminole War, Federal war powers had prevailed over state laws on slave property.

In 1842, Adams again examined slavery and war powers on the floor of Congress, this time in the context of possible war with Great Britain. In November 1841, the American ship *Creole* was carrying slaves from Virginia to New Orleans when the people in the "cargo" rebelled, took over the vessel, and sailed it to the Bahama Islands, a British colony. Those who had killed one of the *Creole*'s owners were tried and executed by the colonial authorities, but the British government refused to return the rest of the escapees to the United States and renewed slavery.

On March 21, 1842, the House of Representatives began to debate possible responses to the *Creole* incident, including a declaration of war. Congressman Joshua Giddings, an abolitionist Whig from Ohio, proposed a series of resolutions that turned the debate in an unexpected direction. The South maintained that slavery was a state issue, to be governed solely by the internal law of each state. Very well, Giddings would take them at their word. If slavery existed only because it was sanctioned by state law, then, according to Giddings's resolutions, it ceased to exist wherever state law did not reach. When the slaves on the *Creole* rebelled, the vessel was on the high seas, in international waters. Having passed beyond the jurisdiction of any U.S. state, the rebels were no longer slaves, but persons being held against their will by superior force. At that time and place they had the natural right to use force to gain their freedom.

In the end, Giddings withdrew his resolutions, but this did not stop the House from censuring him for having offered them. To protect his Southern colleagues from having to listen to more of his distasteful opinions on slavery, Giddings was even prevented from speaking in his own defense before the vote on censure.[25]

Nevertheless, within a month they were forced to hear equally disturbing opinions on slavery from Mr. Adams during debate about possible war with Britain and Mexico. Ironically, Adams made these remarks while purporting to explain why he would have voted *against* one of the Giddings resolutions had it not been withdrawn. The resolution he opposed would have declared that "the slave States have the exclusive right of consultation on the subject of slavery." That, he explained, was not sound constitutional doctrine:

> I believe that, so long as the slave States are able to sustain their institutions without going abroad or calling upon other parts of the Union to aid them or act on the subject, so long I will consent never to interfere. I have said this, and I repeat it; but if they come to the free States, and say to them, You must help us to keep down our slaves, you must aid us in an insurrection and a civil war, then I say that with that call comes full and plenary power to this house and to the Senate over the whole subject. It is a war power. I say it is a war power; and when your country is actually at war, whether it be a war of invasion or a war of insurrection, Congress has power to carry on the war, and must carry it on, according to the laws of war; and by the laws of war an invaded country has all its laws and municipal institutions swept by the board, and martial law takes the place of them. . . . But when the laws of war are in force, what, I ask, is one of those laws? It is this: that when a country is invaded, and two hostile armies are set in martial array, the commanders of both armies have power to emancipate all the slaves in the invaded territory.[26]

This was the speech upon which Senator Sumner most directly relied in telling President Lincoln he could emancipate slaves in a civil war. Since 1836, John Quincy Adams must have studied more deeply the relationship between the war powers and slavery. He no longer referred to the law of nations in general, but rather to a specific branch of that law—the laws of war—as the source of Federal power over slavery. Instead of an ambiguous power to interfere with slavery, he now explicitly claimed a Federal right of emancipation as a weapon of war, even in a war to suppress slave rebellion. It is hard to imagine that Joshua Giddings, had he been allowed to speak, would have said anything more offensive to the South.

Adams's assertion that the laws of war allowed army commanders "to emancipate all the slaves in the invaded territory" was based on his understanding of international customary law. While serving as secretary of state for James Monroe, Adams had become familiar with the precedents for military emancipation through his handling of American claims for slaves freed by British naval forces during the War of 1812. (Indeed, he had pursued these claims so effectively that he would be charged with hypocrisy for asserting the legitimacy of military emancipation in 1842.) During his speech to Congress he cited a case of military emancipation that had occurred while he was secretary of state: "Slavery was abolished in Colombia, first, by the Spanish General Morillo, and, secondly, by the American General Bolivar. It was abolished by virtue of a military command given at the head of the army, and its abolition continues to be law to this day. It was abolished by the laws of war, and not by . . . municipal enactments. . . ."[27]

The incidents to which Adams referred occurred between 1814 and 1816, during the Latin American wars of independence against Spain. King Ferdinand VII sent General Pablo Morillo to present-day Venezuela and Colombia in 1814 in an effort to suppress the movement toward independence. General Morillo initially tried to win the loyalty of the rebellious provinces through leniency to those who were willing to lay down their arms and reaffirm loyalty to the Spanish crown. As part of this policy, Morillo granted freedom to slaves who enlisted in the royal army. By December 1815, Simon Bolivar, one of the primary leaders of the independence movement, had fled to Haiti, where President Alexander Petion provided him with weapons and ammunition and allowed him to recruit Haitian soldiers for a return to South America. In return for this support, the Haitian president made only one request—that

Bolivar free all slaves in the countries that he would liberate. In partial compliance with this obligation, after returning to Venezuela in 1816, Bolivar issued his own emancipation proclamation, offering freedom to slaves (and their families) willing to fight for independence.[28]

Adams exaggerated when he claimed that slavery in the region had been "abolished by virtue of a military command given at the head of the army, and its abolition continues to be law to this day." In fact, slavery there was not finally eliminated until twelve years after he spoke.[29] This in no way undercut the legitimacy of Morillo's and Bolivar's decrees, however, or Adams's use of them as examples of emancipation as a means of warfare.

Morillo's and Bolivar's actions were not unusual, and Adams could have cited other examples from the history of Latin America. Although slavery was not finally abolished in Spanish colonies until the 1880s, Spain had long used emancipation as a weapon against other slave-holding powers. The earliest emancipation proclamation in the Western Hemisphere had been issued by the Spanish government in 1693.[30] During the seventeenth and early eighteenth centuries, Spain claimed that her colony in Florida extended as far north as the Carolinas. Though a formal state of war only occasionally existed between Spain and England in this period, the security of Spanish Florida was directly and continually threatened by the new (and to Spain, illegal) English colonies of South Carolina and Georgia. From the 1680s through the 1730s, relations between Spanish Florida and the Southern English colonies were marked by a hostility often rising to the level of undeclared war.

In 1687, eleven refugees from slavery in South Carolina reached St. Augustine, the Spanish capital of Florida. Seeing an opportunity to weaken his English adversaries while bolstering the strength of his under-populated colony, the Spanish governor offered the refugees freedom and land on his own authority. In compliance with the highly bureaucratic practices of the Spanish Empire, he also forwarded a report of this action to his superiors. Eventually, it reached the court of King Carlos II.

The king not only approved his governor's act, but in 1693 issued a royal decree adopting emancipation of escaped English slaves as an official policy of the empire. "Giving liberty to all," the decree read, ". . . the men as well as the women . . . so that by their example and my liberality others will do the same." During the next seventy years, at least

250 slaves escaped from the Carolinas and Georgia and made it to St. Augustine and freedom. In 1738, as tensions rose between Spain and England, eventually leading to the War of Jenkin's Ear (1739) and the War of the Austrian Succession (1740–1748), the Spanish government organized the escaped slaves as a militia and settled them at Fort Mose, north of St. Augustine. Freed English slaves and their families thus became the primary bulwark of Spanish Florida against English land attack. Their loyalty to the Spanish crown was ensured by the knowledge that capture by British forces would result in certain re-enslavement.[31]

In 1793, Spain used emancipation as a weapon again the French Republic, during Spain's invasion of the French colony on Santo Domingo (today's Haiti). Spanish forces freed and then armed French slaves to fight against their former masters. In response, the French governor abolished slavery in the colony on August 23, 1793, again as a military measure in the war against Spain.[32]

In the eighteenth and early nineteenth centuries, Great Britain used emancipation as a weapon of war even more often than Spain, although slavery remained legal in British colonies until the 1830s. In 1709, for example, a British Royal Navy captain freed and armed thirty-two slaves he had captured from the Spanish, on condition that they fight alongside his men against their former masters.[33] During the Napoleonic Wars, Jose dos Passos, a slave in the Portuguese colony of Brazil, was captured and freed by a British privateer (a privately owned warship licensed to prey on enemy commerce and property). His case is unusual in that he had the audacity to return to Brazil after the restoration of peace, and was employed as a blacksmith in the royal stables. In 1817, he successfully petitioned the king of Portugal for a letter declaring him to be a free man as a result of his capture by the British.[34]

During the American Revolution, the royal governor of Virginia, Lord Dunmore, having been driven out of the colony by the rebels, issued a military emancipation proclamation on November 7, 1775. The proclamation offered freedom to Virginia slaves "appertaining to rebels" who were "able and willing to bear arms." Like Abraham Lincoln eighty years later, Lord Dunmore declared that the proclamation had been issued on "absolute necessity," and under authority of "martial law." Within a week, 500 Virginia slaves had fled to the British. By December 1, 1775, Lord Dunmore was able to muster 300 former slaves into royal service as Loyalist militia.[35]

Less than four years later, Lord Dunmore's policy was extended to all the rebellious American colonies. On June 30, 1779, Sir Henry Clinton, the British commander in chief in North America, issued the "Philipsburg Proclamation," offering freedom to slaves of rebel masters provided the males were willing to join the British military.[36] In 1783, when British forces evacuated New York, Charleston, and Savannah, 14,000 African Americans went with them. In New York City, an official registry of former slaves entitled to freedom under the Philipsburg Declaration included 3,000 names. A recent history has concluded that as many as 100,000 slaves may have gained freedom during the American Revolution by escaping to the British.[37] Great Britain used emancipation against the United States again during the War of 1812, giving rise to the American claims for compensation Adams had asserted while secretary of state.

By the 1840s, then, emancipation of slaves had often been used as a weapon of war in the Americas, both offensively and defensively. Offensive emancipation decrees usually offered freedom to enslaved persons still under the control of the enemy. They were used to wage both economic warfare, by reducing the resources supporting the enemy's war effort, and psychological warfare, by influencing a disaffected minority in the enemy's midst to desert to the other side. Such decrees might also increase the military resources of the emancipating side, if escaped enemy slaves were drawn upon as a new source of recruits for military service or other labor in support of the war effort. Examples of offensive emancipation decrees include the seventeenth-century Spanish decree aimed at English slaves in the Carolinas, and the British decrees aimed at American slaves during the Revolution and in the War of 1812.

Defensive emancipation decrees, granting freedom to the emancipating belligerent's own slaves, were usually issued in response to, and to counteract the effects of, an enemy's offensive decree. They were an effort to retain slaves' loyalty and to increase their usefulness in support of the war, often by offering them freedom in exchange for military service. The French emancipation decree on Santo Domingo, for example, was issued in response to the offensive emancipation policy of invading British and Spanish forces. Later, Simon Bolivar's emancipation decree, with its promise of freedom conditioned on acceptance of military service in the revolutionary cause by male slaves of military age, was issued in response to the offensive emancipation decrees of the Spanish general Morillo.

John Quincy Adams's argument that U.S. governmental powers

were vastly expanded in time of war soon found direct application in the 1846–1848 war between the United States and Mexico. In 1846, the U.S. Army was poorly equipped, from a legal standpoint, for foreign operations. The Articles of War, the military code enacted by Congress in 1806, only authorized courts-martial to punish soldiers for uniquely military offenses, like desertion or disobedience of orders. Soldiers accused of murder, rape, theft, or other ordinary crimes were to be turned over to local civilian authorities—obviously impractical for an army operating outside the United States in hostile territory.

Courts-martial similarly had little authority over the inhabitants of enemy territory. Article of War 56 authorized the death penalty for anyone providing the enemy with "money, victuals or ammunition," and article 57 provided the same penalty for anyone "holding correspondence with, or giving intelligence to, the enemy, either directly or indirectly." In addition, section 2 of the act establishing the Articles of War authorized general courts-martial to punish "persons not citizens of, or owing allegiance to," the United States who were found "lurking as spies in or about" military installations in time of war. U.S. courts-martial had no jurisdiction over any other crimes or acts of resistance, violent or otherwise, by members of the enemy civilian population, even though as a practical matter no invading army could ignore the killing of its soldiers or the theft or destruction of its supplies by the local populace.

In 1846, knowing that the government planned to invade Mexican territory in the event of war, the Commanding General of the Army, Winfield Scott, requested that Congress expand court-martial jurisdiction over crimes by both American soldiers and enemy civilians. His request was ignored. In 1847 these problems became more than academic for General Scott when he took the field in command of an expeditionary force to capture Mexico City. Soon faced with the need to deal with crimes against Mexican civilians by his soldiers, as well as offenses against his army by the civilian population, he came up with a unique and creative solution—special military courts based solely on executive authority rather than on any act of Congress.

General Scott had studied law before entering the army, and his reasoning was similar to Justice Story's approach to war powers. The Constitution, in this view, gave the president (and through him the officers of the army) all necessary authority to conduct war successfully. In enemy territory, this included the need to punish hostile acts against the army, as well as crimes against the local population by American troops that might incite such hostility. Hence an American commander in the field could convene ad hoc military tribunals to deal with these offenses. To distinguish them from courts-martial convened under the Articles of War, Scott referred to these tribunals by the French term "military commissions." (He was quite proud of his knowledge of European military thought, and usually traveled with a small library of French military treatises.) Consisting of three or more officers, military commissions under Scott generally followed the same procedural rules as courts-martial. General Zachary Taylor and other field commanders in the Mexican War also used military commissions to govern the vast occupied territory conquered from Mexico.[38] President James Polk's administration was somewhat uneasy with these developments, but tolerated them as a necessary price of victory.

In 1849, John Quincy Adams's argument that an American government's war powers extended to internal conflicts as well as international wars received support from an unlikely source—Chief Justice Roger Taney's opinion in a case arising from an insurrection in Rhode Island. In 1841, the Rhode Island government was still operating under an old British colonial charter going back to 1663. Citizens frustrated with the government's refusal to adopt a more modern and democratic frame of government finally took matters into their own hands. Opponents of the old charter convened a convention that drafted and adopted a new constitution, under which a governor and other officers were purportedly elected. For a time, two parallel governments existed in Rhode Island, until the governor and legislature of the old charter government declared martial law and called out the militia to suppress their rivals as rebels. The U.S. government did not become directly involved, but President John Tyler did declare that he was ready to use Federal forces to support the old charter government if requested.

The "governor" under the new constitution later sued a state militia officer for trespass and false arrest, and the case eventually came before the U.S. Supreme Court. After deciding that the president's recognition of the charter government made it the legitimate government of Rhode Island, Chief Justice Roger Taney examined whether the Federal courts could review the use of military force by a state government against persons in rebellion against it:

> The State itself must determine what degree of force the cri-
> sis demands. And if the government of Rhode Island deemed

the armed opposition so formidable and so ramified through-out the State as to require the use of its military force and the declaration of martial law, we see no ground upon which this court can question its authority. *It was a state of war, and the established government resorted to the rights and usages of war to maintain itself, and to overcome the unlawful opposition.* And in that state of things, the officers engaged in its military service might lawfully arrest anyone who, from the information before them, they had reasonable grounds to believe was engaged in the insurrection, and might order a house to be forcibly entered and searched when there were reasonable grounds for suppos-ing he might be there concealed. Without the power to do this, martial law and the military array of the government would be mere parade, and rather encourage attack than repel it.[39]

A state government could resort to all the powers authorized by the law of war to suppress an insurrection. Surely the Federal government would hold similar powers if faced with a rebellion requiring the use of military force.

John Quincy Adams did not live to see this partial vindication of his constitutional theories by the Supreme Court. A passionate oppo-nent of the war with Mexico, he suffered a fatal stroke on the floor of Congress in 1848 while speaking against a resolution congratulating General Scott's army for its victories.[40]

By 1861, then, American leaders had seen constitutional "war pow-ers" successfully invoked to suppress an internal insurrection, to create courts unmentioned in any Federal statute, and to govern vast territories without Congressional authority. They were also familiar with emanci-pation of enemy slaves as a weapon of war through the history of the Revolution, the War of 1812, and the Seminole Wars, as well as through the speeches of John Quincy Adams.

Ironically, Adams was also the source of the most common argu-ment against the legality of emancipation under the laws of war, which offered opponents of emancipation the additional pleasure of present-ing him as a hypocrite. Then as now, the writings of academic experts were an important source of the law of nations, and it was often pointed out that no major writer on the law of war mentioned the right of bel-ligerents to free their enemies' slaves. In the first half of the nineteenth century, American lawyers and courts looking for the rules of the law of nations usually consulted the works of a small group of European lawyers who wrote in the seventeenth and eighteenth centuries, including Hugo Grotius (1538–1645) and Cornelius van Bynkershock (1673–1743) of the Netherlands, and Emmerich de Vattel (1714–1767) of Switzerland. Vattel was the most popular of these authorities with American lawyers and judges, who cited his *Law of Nations* (1758) more than any other work on the subject. Bynkershock and Grotius were the authorities next most frequently cited.[41] If emancipation was a lawful method of warfare, the argument ran, surely it would have been discussed somewhere in the writings of these experts.

As secretary of state during the Russian arbitration of U.S. claims against Great Britain for American slaves freed in the War of 1812, Adams had instructed the U.S. minister to Russia to deny the existence of a general right to free enemy slaves under the laws of war, if the British raised the issue in their arguments to the czar. In support of this position, the U.S. minister was to refer to the lack of scholarly writing supporting such a right.

In the event, the British side never raised this issue, and the czar's decision was based solely on the text of the Treaty of Ghent. Indeed, the czar specifically stated that his decision was not based on any principle of general international law, and thus neither affirmed nor rejected the right of wartime emancipation.[42] (After all, the Imperial Russian government might someday want to use emancipation as a weapon against its Moslem enemies in Central Asia.)

Because the issue was never raised in the arbitration proceedings, the United States never had to officially deny the existence of a right of emancipation in time of war, probably to the relief of both the secretary of state and the American minister in St. Petersburg. The denial of such a right would have flown in the face of the historical use of emancipation by European powers.

The anti-emancipation argument based on the silence of expert writers was little more than pettifoggery. It was true that European legal writers said nothing about the treatment of enemy slaves in war. They said a great deal, however, about the treatment of property belonging to enemy citizens. In the case of *United States v. Brown*,[43] two of the most gifted jurists in American history, Chief Justice John Marshall and Justice Joseph Story, had exhaustively examined the work of Emmerich de Vattel and the other European writers; both had found that all these experts acknowledged the right of a state at war to take ownership of property belonging to enemy citizens, though many also advised their readers that governments should make only a limited use of these powers. Slave owners, in particular, could not deny that, in their view, slaves were merely another form of property, entitled to no greater protection from enemy action in war than any other property. Despite the flaws in their reasoning, however, American opponents of emancipation as a war power could still argue that John Quincy Adams's denial of a right to emancipate was the closest thing the United States had to an "official" position on the issue.[44]

2

The Supreme Court on Private Property and War

Where the laws of war apply, the ordinary civil and criminal laws are swept aside, much as generals Thomas Jesup and Zachary Taylor swept aside local laws on fugitive slaves to ensure that their Seminole captives were treated as prisoners of war. Peacetime law is not to be disregarded in every wartime situation, however. The application of the laws of war focuses primarily on relations between enemies, not persons on the same side. Two nineteenth-century decisions of the U.S. Supreme Court illustrate this distinction.

United States v. Brown[1] arose out of the War of 1812 with England. Immediately before the war, several London merchants had hired the American ship *Emulous* to take 550 tons of pine lumber from Savannah, Georgia, to Plymouth, England. On April 18, 1812, the *Emulous* sailed from Savannah to her home port at New Bedford, Massachusetts, where the lumber was unloaded while the ship underwent repairs. After Congress declared war on England, the owner of the *Emulous*, John Delano, seized the lumber and induced the U.S. attorney for Massachusetts to file suit on behalf of himself and of the United States, asking the court to declare the lumber forfeited to the United States as enemy property. (Presumably, Delano would then claim a suitable reward for having patriotically seized his own customers' property, thus reinforcing the stereotype of the sharp-dealing Yankee trader.) Armitz Brown, who had purchased the British merchants' rights in the lumber, opposed Delano's suit, arguing that the most modern authorities on the law of war opposed confiscating the property of enemy nationals that happened to be in a country's territory at the time its government declared war.

At that time, Supreme Court justices presided over lower Federal courts when the higher tribunal was not in session. At the trial of this case, Joseph Story upheld the seizure of the pine logs as a legitimate war measure. By declaring war on Great Britain, he reasoned, Congress had given the president all the powers necessary to win the war. These powers were defined by the law of nations, which allowed any government at war to confiscate the private property of enemy citizens.

Brown appealed Story's decision to the Supreme Court. There, Chief Justice John Marshall made it clear that he and the other justices agreed with Justice Story that the law of war allowed the seizure and forfeiture of any private property owned by persons living under the control of the enemy government. "Respecting the power of government, no doubt is entertained. That war gives to the sovereign full right to take the persons and confiscate the property of the enemy, wherever found, is conceded. The mitigations of this rigid rule, which the humane and wise policy of modern times has introduced into practice, will more or less affect the exercise of this right, but cannot impair the right itself."[2]

The "humane and wise policy of modern times" to which the chief justice referred had been reflected in the provisions of many European treaties dealing with the problems faced by foreign merchants stranded with their goods in enemy territory at the outbreak of a war. By a strict application of the law of nations as expounded by Chief Justice Marshall, an enemy merchant's goods could be seized and confiscated as soon as a war broke out, even though his sovereign and the ruler of the place where the goods were located had been at peace when he imported them. In the eighteenth and early nineteenth centuries, it was common for treaties between European powers to include clauses allowing merchants in this situation a certain period of time, such as six months, after the outbreak of war to sell or export their goods and return to their home country.

In 1798, the U.S. Congress had addressed this issue as part of a statute dealing with enemy aliens in general. After authorizing the apprehension and detention of enemy aliens during a declared war, the act went on to provide "that aliens resident within the United States . . . shall be allowed, for the recovery, disposal and removal of their goods and effects, and for their departure, the full time which is, or shall be stipulated by any treaty" between their government and the United States. If there was no such treaty, then "the President of the United States may ascertain and declare such reasonable time as may be consistent with the public safety, and according to the dictates of humanity and national hospitality."[3]

Unfortunately, this act did not apply to the British owners of the pine logs in the *Brown* case, because they had never been residents of the United States. Nevertheless, the injustice they faced was very similar to that faced by a U.S.-resident British merchant—both had lawfully acquired private property in the United States in peacetime, and through no fault of their own faced total loss of it as a result of sovereign acts of the British and American governments. The justices of the Supreme Court would naturally be sympathetic to the British property owners in *United States v. Brown.*

In the end, Mr. Brown, representing the interests of those property owners, won the suit. Without denying the sovereign power of the United States to confiscate the property of alien enemies, Chief Justice Marshall nevertheless concluded that under the constitutional scheme of the United States, only Congress could authorize the seizure and forfeiture of enemy private property, at least the seizure of property found in American territory at the commencement of hostilities. No statute authorizing such forfeiture had been passed; indeed, the only statute dealing in any way with enemy alien property seemed to lean in favor of the owners of the pine logs. (Not surprisingly, Justice Story dissented from the Court's decision to reverse his lower-court opinion.) In his opinion for the Court, Chief Justice Marshall also specifically noted that in this case the seizure had not been ordered or approved by the president as part of the government's effort to prosecute the war. This statement would be extremely significant for the U.S. government almost fifty years later.

At the time of the Civil War, the *Brown* decision was still the leading American case on the treatment of enemy private property under the laws of war. Since slaves were regarded as a form of private property, *Brown* stood at the foundation of John Quincy Adams's and Charles Sumner's assertions that the laws of war empowered belligerent governments to emancipate enemy slaves.

In contrast to *Brown* is another Supreme Court decision involving private property in wartime, *Mitchell v. Harmony.*[4] Mr. Harmony was a New York merchant engaged in the overland trade between Missouri and Santa Fe in 1846 when war broke out between the United States and Mexico. On December 14, a U.S. military expedition under the command of Colonel Alexander Doniphan set out from Santa Fe to invade northern Mexico. It was accompanied by a caravan of 300 merchants who hoped to reopen trade with Mexico that had been interrupted by the war. Mr. Harmony joined this group in Santa Fe with his wagons and merchandise, but decided to leave the military column in January 1847 to strike out on his own, even though the expedition was then in the middle of enemy territory. Concerned that Harmony's wagons would be captured by Mexican forces, and foreseeing a military need to use them himself, Colonel Doniphan ordered Lieutenant Colonel David Mitchell to seize the wagons and mules. On February 28, Doniphan used the wagons as part of a mobile fortification in a battle for the city of Chihuahua. Having seen hard service in the war, Harmony's wagons were abandoned by the army when it withdrew from Chihuahua on April 23, 1847.[5] After the war, Harmony sued Mitchell for the value of his wagons, mules, and merchandise, and the case eventually came before the U.S. Supreme Court.

It might be thought that a merchant who voluntarily joined a military force invading enemy territory would assume the risks that he would not be allowed to leave the column without the commanding officer's permission, and that his property might be damaged during combat with the enemy. Whatever the merchant's reasonable expectations in this situation, it might also be thought that an army officer, acting in his official capacity in enemy territory to prevent the wagons from leaving, would not be held personally liable for damage to the merchant's property. Chief Justice Roger Taney, speaking for the Court, would have none of this. Harmony was a U.S. citizen, and under the Fifth Amendment to the Constitution private property could not be taken for public use without just compensation. The army had no legal right to order Lieutenant Colonel Mitchell to seize Harmony's goods, so Mitchell could not use superior orders as a defense. The Supreme Court upheld a judgment against Mitchell for more than $90,000 in damages, plus $5,000 in court costs.

The furthest Chief Justice Taney would go to acknowledge that military considerations might have some impact on the property rights of citizens was to concede that private property might be taken for public service, or to prevent it from falling into enemy hands, where "the danger is immediate, and impending; or the necessity urgent for the public service, such as will not admit of delay." In such a case, the officer would not be personally liable, but still "the government is bound to make full compensation to the owner."[6]

Thus, under the laws of war, the U.S. government and its military arms were not required to respect any rights of the owner of private property belonging to an enemy national. Private property owned by an American citizen, however, must be fully respected, even in wartime, because—except in the case of civil war—the laws of war would not apply to relations between a government and its own people. If military necessity required seizure or destruction of American property, the government must still compensate the owner.

The laws of war override civilian law in other important respects, too, perhaps most radically in the form of the combatant privilege. The combatant privilege allows soldiers in war to commit acts against their armed enemies that, under civilian criminal law, would be murder and mayhem. In crucial respects, it differs from the similar privileges that the criminal law recognizes for civilians using force in self-defense against violent criminals, or for police officers using reasonable force to arrest such criminals or to stop a crime in progress. Civilian criminal law distinguishes between the *lawful* use of force, in self-defense or to make an arrest, and the *unlawful* use of force by criminals. Under the law of war, on the other hand, the combatant privilege extends to both sides in an armed conflict. As one Civil War general explained the matter to his officers in early 1862, "a soldier duly enrolled and authorized to act in a military capacity in the enemy's service is not . . . individually responsible for the taking of human life in battle, siege, etc."[7] In April 1863, the U.S. government issued a summary of the laws and usages of war for the use and guidance of Union forces. This document, widely known as the "Lieber Code" after the Columbia University professor who headed its drafting committee, explained the rule as follows: "So soon as a man is armed by a sovereign government and takes the soldier's oath of fidelity, he is a belligerent; his killing, wounding, or other warlike acts are not individual crimes or offenses."[8]

Another difference between the two legal regimes concerns the degree of force that may lawfully be used. Under peacetime civil law, only reasonable force may be used in self-defense or law enforcement. Deadly force may be used only as a last resort, and depending on the circumstances, a warning may be required first. Under the law of war, on the other hand, armed enemy combatants may always be attacked with deadly force. There was no requirement to wound rather than kill, or to cease attacking an enemy army in retreat. By the period of the Civil War, warning the enemy before an attack would be considered folly, and a successful surprise attack would represent the pinnacle of military skill.

During the Civil War, the United States eventually decided to fully apply the laws and customs of war to its dealings with the Confederate forces, and thereafter no effort was made, either before or during the conflict, to apply civil criminal statutes to individual Confederate soldiers or sailors for acts of war. In theory, the crime of treason was treated somewhat differently, in that the Federal government insisted that once the Southern rebellion had been suppressed, individual Confederate officials and officers could be punished as traitors, even though they had been treated as lawful combatants during the war.[9] Before the end of hostilities, however, application of the laws of war to Confederate prisoners of war would prevent their being tried for treason. In early 1862, after Confederate general Simon Bolivar Buckner of Kentucky had surrendered to the U.S. Army, the pro-Union government of his home state indicted him for treason against the state. Secretary of War Edwin Stanton and his subordinates went to considerable trouble to ensure that Buckner was kept in Federal custody as a prisoner of war and not surrendered to Kentucky authorities.[10]

The law of war affected the right to personal liberty in other ways as well. Although captured enemy combatants could not be punished for killing, wounding, or causing other destruction during battle, they could be detained as prisoners of war. Prisoners of war are not held as punishment, but only to prevent or delay their further participation in hostilities. They could therefore be held without trial until the end of the war, and by custom they had rights not accorded to nineteenth-century convicts or culprits being held for trial. In 1861, Quartermaster General Montgomery Meigs reminded Secretary of War Simon Cameron that "prisoners of war are entitled to proper accommodations, to courteous and respectful treatment, to one ration a day and to consideration according to rank."[11]

The right to hold and confine prisoners of war necessarily included the power to release them before the end of hostilities, and to dictate the conditions of release. In the eighteenth and early nineteenth centuries, prisoners taken in European and American wars were routinely released from detention through the mechanisms of parole and exchange.[12] Although the two institutions intermeshed in practice, in theory they were fundamentally different.

Parole was a transaction between an individual prisoner of war and the official military authority holding him captive. The prisoner, in exchange for freedom or less-restrictive conditions of captivity, promised not to engage in specified activity, such as renewed military service in the war or attempting to escape. This promise was often committed to writing and signed by the prisoner.

Although parole was an agreement between the individual prisoner and the government detaining him, the terms and effects of such agreements could be affected by arrangements between the officials of the contending powers. During the War of 1812, for example, the governments of the United States and Great Britain agreed to the following standard format for the documents to be signed by any prisoners allowed to return home on parole:

> Whereas, [name], agent for the care and custody of prisoners of war at ——, has granted me the undersigned prisoner described on the back hereof permission to return to [name of prisoner's country] upon condition that I give my parole of honor that I will not enter into any naval, military or other service whatever against the [name of capturing power] or any of the dominions thereunto belonging, or against any powers at peace with [the capturing power] until I shall have been regularly exchanged, and that I will surrender myself if required by the agent of the government at such place and at such time as may be appointed in case my exchange shall not be effected. And I will until exchanged give notice from time to time of my place of residence. Now in consideration of my enlargement I do hereby declare that I have given my parole of honor accordingly and that I will keep it inviolably.
>
> Given under my hand at —— this — day of ——, in the year of our Lord 18—.

Early in the U.S. Civil War, Confederate paroles of Union prisoners often followed this format as well. This formula was important to the U.S. government because, under these terms, the prisoner only agreed not to engage in any military service against the Confederacy. The United States could therefore use such paroled prisoners of war against hostile Indians on the frontier, or to engage in any other military duties not involving hostilities against the secessionists. In the summer of 1862, however, the U.S. and Confederate military authorities entered into an agreement, known as the "Dix-Hill Cartel," to regulate future parole and exchange of prisoners. Under this cartel, paroled prisoners were precluded from engaging in any military service until released from parole, thus ending the practice of sending paroled troops to serve on the frontier.[13]

A prisoner caught violating his parole, usually by being recaptured while participating in military operations forbidden by its terms, was subject to punishment under the law of war. It was often asserted that death was the appropriate punishment for parole violation, though this appears to have been rarely carried out in practice.[14]

An exchange, unlike a parole, was a transaction between opposing governments or military authorities, under which each agreed to release specific prisoners from custody (or from the terms of parole) in exchange for the release of an equivalent number of prisoners held by the enemy. Exchanges often took into account the military rank of the prisoners, in an effort to ensure that each side received the same "value." Thus a major would be exchanged for another major, a sergeant for a sergeant, and so on. Only rarely would both sides hold equal numbers of prisoners of the same military rank, so agreements, like the Dix-Hill Cartel, were often concluded by setting out agreed equivalent values for each rank. During the American Revolution, for example, the Continental army and the British army agreed in December 1779 that in future exchanges a captain would be exchanged for 16 private soldiers, a major for 28 privates, a colonel for 100, and a major general for 327.[15]

In the late eighteenth century, the fanatically egalitarian government of Revolutionary France tried, unsuccessfully, to eliminate all distinctions of rank in prisoner exchanges.[16] That the French policy nevertheless had some impact on international practice can be seen in the exchange cartel negotiated between the United States and Great Britain in the War of 1812. Under this agreement, the value of officers had markedly declined since the American Revolution: a captain was now worth only 6 private soldiers, a major 8, a colonel 15, and a major general would be exchanged for a mere 30 privates.[17] This agreement later served as a model during negotiation of the Dix-Hill Cartel.

Another implication of applying the laws of war should be noted, since it had an important impact on both the conduct of the Civil War and the development of American constitutional law. The laws and usages of war recognized a wide range of offenses that were unknown in civilian criminal law. One of these new offenses, parole violation, has already been mentioned. Other offenses unique to the laws of war included spying, mistreatment of prisoners of war, abuse of the flag of truce, and unlawful, or unprivileged, belligerency. Under the law of the United States, none of these activities would be regarded as a crime by any state or federal civilian court. During the war with Mexico, both Lieutenant General Scott and Major General Taylor turned to the use of military commissions largely because they needed to find some regular judicial process for the trial and punishment of these and other offenses under the laws of war.

Similar problems persist to this day. In the summer of 2003, the U.S. government announced its intention to try two British subjects, Feroz Abbasi and Mozam Begg, by military commission for alleged illegal belligerency during the conflict in Afghanistan. The British public reaction was extremely negative, and 200 members of Parliament signed a protest demanding that the suspects be returned to England for trial. One of the primary difficulties facing the British government in resolving this dispute was that, although the United States intended to charge Mr. Abbasi and Mr. Begg with violation of the law of war, there was no comparable offense recognized in British civilian criminal law.[18]

The offense of unprivileged belligerency became especially important during the Civil War, because it was closely related to the phenomenon of guerrilla warfare. As already noted, when the law of war applied, members of organized military units, fighting openly, in uniform, under the authority of the enemy's government, could not be punished under ordinary criminal law for the injury and destruction they caused during combat. Persons who took part in hostilities without meeting these requirements, however, were not only denied immunity from ordinary criminal law, but could also be punished under the laws of war for the offense of unlawful belligerency.

Two forms of unlawful belligerency were frequently encountered by both sides during the Civil War. The first involved participation in combat by persons who were not members of officially authorized Union or Confederate military commands. By a General Order issued on January 1, 1862, Major General Henry Halleck, then in command of the U.S. Army's Department of Missouri, explained the rule as follows:

> While the code of war gives certain exemption to a soldier regularly in the military service of an enemy it is a well-established

principle that insurgents not militarily organized under the laws of the State . . . are not entitled to such exemptions; such men are not legitimately in arms and the military name and garb which they have assumed cannot give a military exemption to the crimes which they may commit. They are in a legal sense mere freebooters and banditti and are liable to the same punishment which was imposed upon guerrilla bands by Napoleon in Spain, and by Scott in Mexico.[19]

That punishment, imposed by sentence of a military commission, was death.

Article 82 of the Lieber Code—a codification of the law of war issued by the U.S. government in 1863 for the use of Union forces, as mentioned above—explained the rule in more detail:

Men, or squads of men, who commit hostilities, whether by fighting, or inroads for destruction or plunder, or by raids of any kind, without commission, without being part and portion of the organized hostile army, and without sharing continuously in the war, but who do so with intermitting returns to their homes and avocations, or with the occasional assumption of the semblance of peaceful pursuits, divesting themselves of the character or appearance of soldiers—such men, or squads of men, are not public enemies, and, therefore, if captured, are not entitled to the privileges of prisoners of war, but shall be treated summarily as highway robbers or pirates.[20]

This rule was based on more than a stuffy prejudice of West Point–trained regulars against amateur soldiers. It also reflected the need to protect civilians and other noncombatants against abuse. In any country, soldiers who are part of an official military organization are subject to military discipline, and their superiors can be held ultimately responsible for looting or other crimes against the civilian population. Combatants who are not members of an authorized armed force are much more likely to be, or to become, "highway robbers or pirates" in fact as well as in the eyes of the law.

Of course, it was not always easy for combatants operating behind enemy lines to prove that they were part of a properly authorized and organized military unit, especially in the chaotic conditions of the Civil

War. Even if a person accused of being an unlawful combatant could establish official membership in the enemy's forces, that might not be enough. Consider the trial of Captain John W. Owen, for example.[21] Owen was brought before a military commission at Danville, Missouri, on January 28, 1862, charged with destroying military telegraph lines, railroads, and railroad bridges behind Union lines, "contrary to the laws and customs of war in like cases."[22] Evidence for the defense indicated that Owen had joined a company raised by a Confederate recruiting officer, had been sworn into Confederate service, and was elected captain of the company by the men. When captured, he claimed that the destruction of property with which he was charged had been ordered by General Sterling Price of the pro-Confederate Missouri State Guard.

There was also evidence, however, that Owen and his company did not remain continually under arms. Rather, they returned to their homes after it was decided they could not reach General Price's main force, and came together again only when Price ordered Confederate soldiers behind enemy lines in Missouri to burn railroad bridges and destroy other property of military use. This evidence suggested the existence of a second ground for regarding Owen as an unlawful combatant—that he carried out hostile acts while posing as an ordinary civilian. In the words of the Lieber Code, Captain Owen and his men were engaged in "intermitting returns to their homes and avocations, . . . with the occasional assumption of the semblance of peaceful pursuits, divesting themselves of the character or appearance of soldiers." Owen was convicted and sentenced to death.

In European wars, the wearing of a military uniform was traditionally the primary key to distinguishing lawful from unlawful combatants—an armed man captured in uniform was assumed to be entitled to prisoner of war treatment, while a combatant in civilian clothing was assumed to be an unlawful belligerent. Throughout the Civil War, however, the Confederate army in particular had difficulty supplying its men with uniforms. The real issue, though, was whether the captive had effectively distinguished himself from the civilian population during combat operations, or whether he had attempted to escape discovery and capture by "the occasional assumption of the semblance of peaceful pursuits," to blend in with the civilian population.

About a month after the trial of Captain Owen, Colonel Ebenezer Magoffin, also of the Missouri State Guard, was brought to trial in St. Louis for parole violation and unlawful belligerency.[23] The latter charge arose from the death of a Union cavalry sergeant during a fire fight with Magoffin's State Guards, some of whom, including the colonel, were wearing civilian clothing.

Magoffin presented a forceful defense to this charge. He offered evidence that, in the military confusion of 1861–1862, many soldiers, including members of the pro-Union Missouri Home Guard, fought without uniforms. He also pointed out that he was widely known to be a Confederate officer and had been on active service almost continually. Whatever clothing he may have been wearing during the fight, he had not "assumed the semblance of peaceful pursuits" in order to conceal his character as a soldier. Indeed, he argued, why would the Federal authorities have offered him parole as a Confederate officer unless they knew he was one? The military commission acquitted Colonel Magoffin of unlawful belligerency, but convicted him of parole violation, a decision later appealed to President Lincoln.

The Owen and Magoffin cases were two of many trials by U.S. military commissions in Missouri during 1861–1862. General Sterling Price, CSA, refused to remain silent while his soldiers were condemned as "freebooters and banditti" for operating behind enemy lines. Writing to the Union commander, Major General Halleck, on January 12, 1862, Price argued both that men carrying out sabotage on his orders should be treated as prisoners of war, and, rather inconsistently, that if they were to be tried for these acts, it should be before civilian courts applying peacetime Missouri criminal law.

> I have obtained information that individuals and parties of men specially appointed and instructed by me to destroy railroads, culverts and bridges by tearing them up, burning, &c., have been arrested and subjected to a general court-martial for alleged crimes which all the laws of warfare heretofore recognized by the civilized world have regarded as distinctly lawful and proper. I have learned that such persons when tried, if convicted of the offense or offenses as stated, are viewed as lawful subjects for capital punishment.
>
> . . . It is necessary that we understand each other and have some guiding knowledge of that character of warfare which is to be waged by our respective governments. . . .
>
> Do you intend to regard members of this army as persons deserving death whenever and wherever they may be captured

or will you extend the recognized rights of prisoners of war . . . ? Do you regard—and state as such the law governing your army—the destruction of important roads, transportation facilities, &c., for military purposes as the legal right of a belligerent power? Do you intend to regard men whom I have specially dispatched to destroy roads, burn bridges, tear up culverts, &c., as amenable to an enemy's court-martial or will you have them to be tried as usual by the proper authorities according to the statutes of the State?[24]

General Halleck was himself an authority on international law, and rejected General Price's claims in a letter dated January 22. He sarcastically pointed out that Price's men were unlawful belligerents because they were acting under false pretenses, not because of their lack of authority or official recognition.

Where "individuals and parties of men" violate the laws of war they will be tried and if found guilty will certainly be punished whether acting under your "special appointment and instructions" or not. You must be aware, general, that no orders of yours can save from punishment spies, marauders, robbers, incendiaries, guerrilla bands, &c., who violate the laws of war. You cannot give immunity to crime.

But let us fully understand each other on this point. If you send armed forces wearing the garb of soldiers and duly organized and enrolled as legitimate belligerents to destroy railroads, bridges, &c., as a military act we shall kill them if possible in open warfare, or if we capture them we shall treat them as prisoners of war. But it is well understood that you have sent numbers of your adherents in the garb of peaceful citizens and under false pretenses through our lines into Northern Missouri to rob and destroy the property of Union men and to burn and destroy railroad bridges thus endangering the lives of thousands. . . . Moreover peaceful citizens of Missouri quietly working on their farms have been instigated by your emissaries to take up arms as insurgents and to rob and plunder and to commit arson and murder. They do not even act under the garb of soldiers but under false pretenses and in the guise of peaceful citizens.

You certainly will not pretend that men guilty of such

crimes although "specially appointed and instructed" by you are entitled to the rights and immunities of ordinary prisoners of war. If you do will you refer me to a single authority on the laws of war which recognizes such a claim?[25]

Finally, it should be noted that when the law of war applied to a conflict, custom allowed the military commanders on each side to communicate with each other on purely military matters, and even to conclude military-to-military agreements, with no political significance attached. Such agreements might include temporary truces to gather the wounded after a battle, or the prisoner exchange cartels discussed above. Traditionally, these communications had been conducted through the use of the flag of truce by messengers of each side.

This custom has also survived beyond the nineteenth century, and allows parties at war to conclude mutually advantageous agreements at the military level without adverse political consequences. The Arab–Israeli wars of 1948, 1956, 1967, and 1973 all ended with purely military-to-military agreements to cease fighting and exchange prisoners, without compromising the refusal of most Arab states to recognize the state of Israel. The Korean War of 1950–1953 also ended with a solely military armistice and prisoner exchange. During the war in Iraq in 2003, U.S. forces reached a temporary cease-fire agreement with an Iranian rebel group, operating on Iraqi territory, that was officially regarded as terrorist by the U.S. government.[26]

Although military-to-military agreements were supposed to have no political impact on the legal status of the parties to a conflict, during the Civil War such agreements were a sensitive matter to the Lincoln administration, which wanted to avoid according any further recognition to the Confederate government. When the president declared a blockade of rebel ports in 1861, he inadvertently accorded the Confederates the status of belligerents in international law. Having stumbled once, the administration wanted to avoid doing so again.[27] This policy lasted until the end of the war, and was most clearly set out in a telegram from the secretary of war to General Ulysses S. Grant in 1864, in response to possible peace feelers from General Robert E. Lee. "The President directs me to say to you that he wishes you to have no conference with General Lee unless it be for the capitulation of Gen. Lee's army, or on some minor, and purely, military matter. He instructs me to say that you are not to decide, discuss or confer upon any political question. Such questions the President holds in his own hands; and will submit them to no military conferences or conventions. . . ."[28]

Senator Sumner therefore had solid grounds for his assertion, in the spring of 1861, that President Lincoln could use his war powers to emancipate the slaves. The international law of war was commonly considered a proper measure of the wartime powers of the Federal government, and offering freedom to the enemy's slaves had been a standard practice in the colonial wars of European powers.

Sumner was not alone in the opinion that after the South fired on Fort Sumter, the president had the power to free slaves in the rebellious states. Reportedly, the White House received numerous letters in this period urging the president to use the emancipation weapon. When Congress reconvened in July, Senator Samuel C. Pomeroy of Kansas introduced a bill instructing the president to issue an emancipation proclamation; this was too radical a step for his colleagues, and it did not pass.[29] Even Alexander Stephens, later vice president of the Confederacy, warned the Georgia secession convention that the South risked military emancipation in the event of war with the United States.[30]

Nevertheless, in 1861 there was real danger that such a measure would not withstand challenge in the Federal courts when peace returned. Roger Taney was still chief justice of the United States. In 1856, in the *Dred Scott* case, he had declared that the rights of slaveholders in their human property must be respected by the Federal government under the Fifth Amendment to the Constitution. Five years earlier, in the case of *Mitchell v. Harmony,* he had held an army officer personally liable for the value of property taken, for military use, from a fellow American citizen, despite the officer having acted under orders from his military superior. It was not at all clear how, in a civil war between Americans, Chief Justice Taney's Supreme Court would regard the freeing of enemy slaves by the United States. Would such an act be viewed as the lawful taking of enemy property, under the laws of war as declared by Chief Justice Marshall in 1814? Or would it be seen as the unlawful taking of an American citizen's property, as in *Mitchell v. Harmony?* If the courts found it to be the latter, then issuing a legally defective emancipation proclamation would not only endanger the newfound freedom of slaves who had sought protection from the U.S. Army; it could also expose individual army officers to successful lawsuits by slaveholders, claiming the value of any slaves permanently lost, or the value of the lost labor of those who were recaptured.

Lincoln was forcefully reminded of this in late 1862 when a Kentucky slave owner sued Colonel William Utley of the 22nd Wisconsin Regiment for refusing to return a young slave who had taken refuge in the regiment's camp. Colonel Utley was then on the horns of a legal dilemma. Although Kentucky law required him to return the refugee to his owner, Congress had amended the army's Articles of War to prohibit military officers from returning any fugitive slave to his or her master, subject to punishment by a court-martial.[31] When the case was brought to the president's attention, Lincoln personally appealed to the slave owner to settle the suit and offered him "any sum not exceeding five hundred dollars."[32] The owner, a prominent lawyer, refused this offer because he wanted to make the point that Utley was legally in the wrong, at least under Kentucky law. He pursued the case after the war and obtained a judgment against Colonel Utley for $908.06 (plus court costs) in 1871, more than five years after slavery had been abolished throughout the United States by constitutional amendment. Two years later, Congress appropriated funds to reimburse Colonel Utley.[33] In 1861 and 1862, however, there was no way President Lincoln could be certain that Congress would reimburse Federal officers in every similar case in the future, particularly if the Republicans lost control of either house.

In deciding whether and how to issue an emancipation proclamation, Lincoln had to consider not only its political impact in the slave-holding border states, but also the possible financial impact on the officers of his own army if the proclamation was overturned in the courts. This was an aspect of the emancipation issue that Senator Sumner and Lincoln's other abolitionist critics do not appear to have considered.

3

Criminal Conspiracy or War?

In the summer of 1861, it was not clear whether the Lincoln administration wanted any of the laws of war to apply to its relations with the rebels. And the president could hardly claim to use powers granted him by the laws of war if those laws did not apply. History had provided Lincoln with two models for effectively confronting a rebellion with military force. President Andrew Jackson, whose portrait Lincoln kept in his office at the White House, had threatened force against South Carolina in the Nullification Crisis of 1832–1833. Earlier, President George Washington had mobilized and led a force of federalized militia to put down the Whiskey Rebellion of 1794.

Parson Weems's biography of Washington was one of the first books Lincoln had read, and like most of his countrymen he held a special reverence for the first president. More significantly, he often identified his situations and problems with those of Washington. When leaving Springfield, Illinois, to assume the presidency, he told his fellow townsmen that the task before him was "greater than that which had rested upon Washington."[1] In his first message to Congress on July 4, 1861, Lincoln stressed that the government of the Union had been "made by Washington," and that its "good old" Constitution, unlike that of the Confederacy, had been "signed by Washington."[2] His proclamation calling 75,000 militia into Federal service after the fall of Fort Sumter explicitly relied on the same statute Washington had used in 1794. "From the very start of his political career," one Lincoln scholar has noted, "Lincoln had almost impudently placed himself squarely on the side of America's all-purpose hero."[3]

The Whiskey Rebellion that Washington suppressed grew out of a 1791 Federal excise tax on the distilling of whiskey. This tax, of four cents per gallon, caused "enormous financial hardship" to farmers in the mountainous western counties of Pennsylvania and Virginia. With only the most primitive means of transportation available in those frontier regions, farmers had little choice but to convert most of their crops into whiskey, a commodity much more easily taken to market than bulk grain. The "epicenter" of resistance to the tax was in Western Pennsylvania.[4] When the resistance became violent in the summer of 1794, the president called on the governors of Maryland, New Jersey, Pennsylvania, and Virginia to provide 13,000 militia to suppress the insurgents.

Today, the Whiskey Rebellion is considered a minor episode in the history of the early Republic. At the time, however, President Washington saw it as a major crisis for the new U.S. government. Like his successor in the Secession Crisis of 1861, Washington believed the Whiskey Rebellion raised the fundamental issue of the legitimacy of majority rule. The question at stake, he declared to the public, was nothing less than "whether a small proportion of the United States shall dictate to the whole Union, and, at the expense of those who desire peace, indulge a desperate ambition."[5] The insurgents, he had been advised, were guilty of acts that amounted to treason, "being overt acts of levying War against the United States."[6] In suppressing the rebellion by military force, President Washington, like President Lincoln sixty-seven years later, saw himself fulfilling his "high and irresistible duty" of taking care "that the laws be faithfully executed."[7] Washington's crisis, however, was resolved without bloodshed. The Whiskey Rebellion collapsed in the face of overwhelming Federal forces marching into western Pennsylvania, combined with liberal use of executive clemency. When Pittsburgh was occupied on November 16, the crisis was essentially over. Washington had never had to declare fellow Americans to be national enemies who should be dealt with under the laws of war rather than the Constitution. To the contrary, he had specifically instructed the troops that while they were to "combat and subdue" all those who had taken up arms against the government, they also had a duty to "aid and support the civil magistrate in bringing offenders to justice."[8] Washington's forces were engaged in law enforcement, not war.

The Nullification Crisis of 1832–1833 was, if anything, an even weaker precedent for applying the law of war to domestic rebels. In late November 1832, a South Carolina state convention, acting on states' rights constitutional theories developed by John C. Calhoun, declared the Federal Tariff Acts of 1828 and 1832 to be null and void within South Carolina. The nullification decision was not to take effect until

February 1, 1833, however, allowing time for cooler heads to seek a compromise.

In anticipation of the nullification, President Jackson had consulted with Major General Winfield Scott, commander of the Eastern Division of the U.S. Army. The president authorized Scott to strengthen the Federal garrisons at Fort Moultrie and Castle Pinckney in Charleston harbor, and to secure the U.S. arsenal at Augusta, Georgia, just across the Savannah River from South Carolina. General Scott went to Charleston to supervise these measures on scene and to prevent the outbreak of premature hostilities between his troops and the prickly South Carolinians. On December 10, the president issued a proclamation denying the existence of a right of nullification, asserting the right of the Federal government to collect its tariffs, and warning South Carolina that he would consider secession to be treason.

The president increased the pressure on South Carolina on January 16, 1833, by asking Congress to enact a force bill, authorizing the use of the army, navy, and militia to enforce the tariff laws. On March 1, Congress passed both the force bill and a compromise tariff bill worked out between senators Henry Clay and John C. Calhoun. The crisis had been averted, without hostilities.[9] Had they occurred, the U.S. forces would have acted under Federal domestic law—the force bill—not the international law of war.

Throughout the Civil War, Lincoln maintained that the Southern states had not seceded, and could not secede, from the Union. In his view, the U.S. government was dealing not with a Confederate government, but rather with a group of rebellious individual citizens, just as in the Whiskey Rebellion.[10] One result of this policy was that the administration was extremely sensitive to any measure that might accord a degree of legitimacy to the Confederate government, or to the rebellious state governments. In principle, the law of war applied to hostilities between independent nations, and applying it, in whole or in part, to the rebels could be another incremental step toward recognition of the Confederacy as a true government. Some of his Radical Republican critics believed Lincoln had already stumbled once in declaring a blockade of Southern ports, since under the law of nations this act had the effect of recognizing the rebels as "belligerents," with whom Britain, France, and other neutrals could deal as a semi-sovereign entity.[11] The administration did not want to do anything that would inadvertently extend even more recognition to the Confederate States of America.

As a matter of personal character, Lincoln may have had real difficulty seeing his fellow citizens as enemies.[12] Throughout 1861, the president and his supporters clung to the belief that most of the Southern people were fundamentally loyal to the Union but had been misled by a small clique of secessionist politicians. If ordinary Southerners were handled with firmness and restraint, they believed, the "mystic chords of memory" binding all Americans together would, in time, reassert themselves, and the insurrection would presumably sputter out as had the Whiskey Rebellion in 1794 and the Nullification movement in 1833. Branding everyone in the South as enemies of the United States, subject to the laws and usages of war, would hardly advance this hoped-for process of reconciliation.

At the beginning of the war, the Federal government faced a dilemma in legal policy. There were good political reasons for the Lincoln administration to apply domestic Federal law to its enemies, as Washington and Jackson had done. On the other hand, the Confederate government used every means at its disposal to press Washington to apply the law of war to the growing conflict. The Confederacy claimed to be a sovereign nation, fighting another sovereign, and it wanted the laws of war to apply to its relations with the U.S. government from the beginning of hostilities. In addition, the constitutional war powers that the president and Congress would need to suppress the rebellion were closely linked to the international laws of war.

Between April and December 1861, the Lincoln administration and its military commanders in the field responded to these pressures by slowly applying more and more of the law of war to their dealings with the rebels. The process was gradual and unpublicized because of the administration's constant concern that according international rights to the Confederates would also grant them an increasing degree of international recognition. Faced with this dilemma, the initial reaction of the Lincoln administration was to follow the course adopted by many other governments confronting hard choices—it tried to avoid taking a clear stand for as long as possible. Although the level of hostilities relentlessly grew in intensity throughout 1861, the Lincoln administration stubbornly refused to make a clear choice between the application of the law of war and that of peacetime Federal law to the rebels. Ironically, this ambiguous policy contributed to the practical application of the law of war by Union commanders in the field. With no clear guidance from Washington on how to respond to flags of truce, or whether to consider captured Confederates as prisoners of war, army and navy officers increasingly turned to the laws and customs that they and their predecessors had applied in earlier wars with Mexico and Great Britain. Army regulations told them how prisoners of war were to be treated; they said nothing about persons under arrest for treason.

The administration's legal ambivalence at this early stage of the Civil War is evident in three decisions taken by President Lincoln soon after the fall of Fort Sumter—the call for militia volunteers, the seizure of arms on the Mississippi River, and the declaration of a blockade. On April 15, 1861, immediately after Major Robert Anderson's surrender of Fort Sumter, the president issued a proclamation under the same statutory authority invoked by President Washington in the Whiskey Rebellion, calling 75,000 militia into Federal service. The declared purpose of this force was to "suppress" certain "combinations" of persons in the seceded states.

What is curious in retrospect is that, following the bombardment of a U.S. Army fort by heavy artillery manned by organized and uniformed military formations, the president did not declare these sinister combinations to be "levying War against" the United States, as treason is defined in the Constitution.[13] Rather, the units of the provisional Confederate army were described as "combinations too powerful to be suppressed by the ordinary course of judicial proceedings, or by the powers vested in the [U.S.] Marshals by law." Once these rebellious combinations had been suppressed, the president stated, the militia would "cause the laws to be duly executed" in the South. This is the language of peacetime law enforcement, not the waging of war. The reader is left with the impression that the 75,000-strong militia force would serve merely as an unusually large and colorfully dressed U.S. marshal's posse.[14]

The proclamation also declared that "the utmost care will be observed . . . to avoid any devastation, any destruction of, *or interference with, property,* or any disturbance of peaceful citizens in any part of the country."[15] The president thereby expressly and publicly rejected Senator Sumner's advice to use the law of war to emancipate the insurgents' slaves. Barely two weeks later, however, Lincoln approved a significant military interference with property, the first hint that the White House knew something more than law enforcement might be needed to deal with the Confederacy.

On April 17, Governor Isham Harris of Tennessee refused the president's call for militia, telegraphing the secretary of war that "Tennessee will not furnish a single man for purpose of coercion, but 50,000, if necessary for the defense of our rights and those of our Southern brethren."[16] Thereafter, Governor Richard Yates of Illinois ordered his militia to seize a Mississippi riverboat, the *C. E. Hillman,* carrying munitions to pro-secession forces in Tennessee. On April 29, with an arrogant tone typical of Southern "fire-eater" politicians, Governor Harris wrote the president to protest that this "interruption of the free navigation of the Mississippi River and the seizure of property belonging to the State of Tennessee and her citizens" was "aggressive," "hostile," and an "outrage." He asked "by what authority the said acts were committed," and whether they were "done by or under the instructions of the Federal Government."[17]

Lincoln tried to draft a logical, lawyerly reply. While acknowledging that he had "no official information" about the incident, he nevertheless approved Governor Yates's action. Reminding Governor Harris that he had refused, "in disrespectful and malicious language," to provide Tennessee's quota of militia to the United States, the president concluded that the seizure logically followed from that refusal. "This Government therefore infers that munitions of War passing into the hands of said Governor, are intended to be used against the United States; and the government will not indulge the weakness of allowing it, so long as it is in it's power to prevent—This Government will not, at present, question, but that the State of Tennessee, by a majority of it's citizens, is loyal to the Federal Union, and the government holds itself responsible in damages for all injuries it may do to any who may prove to be such."[18] The president did not, however, tell Governor Harris what legal authority allowed Governor Yates to order the seizures and justified his own approval of them. Indeed, he could not have done so without resolving the legal and political dilemma in which the administration found itself in April 1861.

Under the American law applicable between loyal citizens, the legality of the seizures was extremely doubtful. Governor Yates and the president had reasonable grounds for suspecting that these munitions would be used against the U.S. government, but that would not necessarily justify their seizure by the military, and without a warrant issued by a judge. In 1851, the Supreme Court had held Lieutenant Colonel David Mitchell personally liable for the seizure and loss of Mr. Harmony's wagons and merchandise, even though Mitchell and his superiors suspected that the property would fall into enemy hands during the war with Mexico. Rejecting Mitchell's argument, Chief Justice Roger Taney had forcefully stated that mere suspicion that goods were bound for the enemy was an insufficient ground for military interference with property protected by the Fifth Amendment. Taney was still chief justice in 1861, and the Illinois officers who seized the *C. E. Hillman* and its cargo risked being held liable to the ship's owners and the State of Tennessee if Governor Harris and his supporters were still considered loyal American citizens.

Lincoln the lawyer-president tried to shield these officers from personal liability by declaring that his government would be "responsible in damages for all injuries it may do to any who may prove to be" loyal citizens. Without an act of Congress behind it, however, this promise was also of doubtful effect. In *Mitchell v. Harmony*, Chief Justice Taney had grudgingly acknowledged that the government, rather than an individual military officer, might be held liable for taking private property to prevent it from falling into enemy hands, but only where "the danger is immediate, and impending; or the necessity urgent for the public service, such as will not admit of delay."[19] Since Lincoln had received no official report on the seizure of the *C. E. Hillman*, he could not know whether this exception applied to the present case.

Only under the law of war, using their powers as commanders in chief of state and Federal forces, respectively, could Governor Yates and President Lincoln have justified the seizure of another state's munitions and a privately owned riverboat. But invoking the law of war would have expressly labeled Governor Harris and his forces as enemies, rebels with whom the United States was at war, which would have directly contradicted the president's statement that he was not questioning the loyalty of Tennessee or its citizens. At this stage, the Lincoln administration was desperately trying to hold in the Union as many border slave states as possible. Labeling Governor Harris and his supporters as enemies might be just the act that would push Tennessee into open secession.

It is not clear whether President Lincoln's reply to Governor Harris was ever sent, since it is available only as an undated and unsigned draft in Lincoln's hand. The president may have realized that any reply to Governor Harris, short of disavowing the seizure, would be taken as another affront, or events may have overtaken the need to send it. Tennessee seceded on June 8, 1861, and in early 1862 Governor Harris fled south before advancing Union armies. The draft does, however, reflect

President Lincoln's early determination not to allow peacetime property law to impede the suppression of the rebellion, even if he could not, as yet, identify a clear legal foundation for this decision. The armies of the Union would respect private property as far as they could, but when there was a clear conflict between property rights and military effectiveness, the president had already made his choice. In a sense, this is the seed from which the Emancipation Proclamation grew.

As mentioned, the Lincoln administration had already been forced, to an extent, to apply the international law of war to its dealings with the rebels. On April 19, the president declared a blockade of the ports in the Confederate states, pursuant to "the laws of the United States and the law of Nations, in such case provided." The term "blockade" carried a definite burden of meaning in international law, and its use meant the United States was claiming certain rights, and recognizing obligations, in its relations with Britain, France, and other neutral nations. Declaring a blockade also meant, however, that the United States was acknowledging the Confederates were "belligerents"—that is, that they had at least a limited international status, short of recognition as an independent nation, while the war continued. This had the effect of according neutral governments the right and the obligation to deal even-handedly with the United States and the Confederate States where military matters were concerned, giving material assistance to neither side.

To avoid recognizing the Confederates as belligerents, the administration had considered the alternative of ordering the closure to international commerce of all ports in the seceded states. Every nation had the sovereign right to establish commercial ports of entry into its territory and to close those ports at will. Since the Federal government viewed secession as illegal and without effect, commerce with Confederate ports was, so the argument ran, still under the sovereign control of the United States. In other words, the administration would have preferred closing Southern ports by using internal U.S. law, not the international law of war.[20]

The problem was that whatever the policy was called, as a practical matter it would have to be enforced by the U.S. Navy in international waters, the "high seas," outside the three-mile limit claimed by the United States. Under international law, warships enforcing a blockade on the high seas had the right to stop and search merchant vessels from neutral nations, and even to seize those that had already violated the blockade or had cargo destined for a blockaded port. No similar rights were recognized to enforce a nation's closure of its own ports. If a warship stopped another country's merchant ships on the high seas to determine whether they were going to or coming from a port closed under national law, it would be violating the internationally recognized freedom of the seas. If the United States tried to enforce the closure of Southern ports by stopping British and French shipping on the high seas, then, those countries would almost certainly go to war to defend their rights. Like it or not, the closure of Confederate ports had to be accomplished through a blockade—that is, by the application of the law of war.

The blockade proclamation rejected the law of war in other relations with the rebel forces. In its preamble, the proclamation noted that the Confederate government (referred to as "a combination of persons, engaged in . . . insurrection") had "threatened to grant pretended letters of marque to authorize the bearers thereof to commit assaults on the lives, vessels, and property of good citizens of the country lawfully engaged in commerce on the high seas and in waters of the United States." A letter of marque was a government license authorizing a privately owned warship, referred to as a "privateer," to prey on enemy merchant vessels, or even on neutral vessels carrying military supplies ("contraband") to the enemy. They were a common institution in European naval warfare from the Middle Ages through the middle of the nineteenth century. Captured merchant ships were to be brought before the courts of the government that had issued the letter of marque for a determination as to whether the capture was proper under international law. If these courts approved the capture, the ship was said to be "condemned as a prize" and was sold. The proceeds of sale were divided between the government, the owners of the privateer, and its crew, according to a formula set by the issuing government.

In its blockade proclamation, however, the Lincoln administration announced that it would refuse to recognize the legitimacy of letters of marque issued by the Confederate government. If any Confederate privateers were captured by U.S. forces, the crew members would be treated as criminals, not prisoners of war: "And I hereby proclaim and declare that if any person under the pretended authority of the said States, or under any other pretense, shall molest a vessel of the United States, or the persons or cargo on board of her, such persons will be held amenable to the laws of the United States for the prevention and punishment of piracy." In retrospect, most historians would view this policy as unwise. As is described later, the government's attempts to actually prosecute Confederate privateers had embarrassing consequences for the Lincoln administration.

What is significant is that, as a logical matter, the declared intention to treat Confederate privateers as pirates was difficult to reconcile with the decision to impose a blockade on Confederate ports. A blockade would be legitimate, and entitled to respect from other nations, only if it had been imposed as a military measure during a war between nations, or in a civil war between a government and an insurgent group recognized as a belligerent power. If the Confederacy was a belligerent, then under the law of war it had the power to exercise belligerent rights. These rights included the issuance of letters of marque.

Strictly speaking, under the international law of the time, the United States could punish its own citizens for treason, piracy, murder, or any other offense against U.S. law, and as far as other nations were concerned, the Congress could define those crimes however it wished. However, the Federal criminal statute punishing piracy, at that time and today, defines the offense as "the crime of piracy as defined by the law of nations,"[21] and under the law of nations, privateersmen acting under a letter of marque issued by a recognized belligerent would not be pirates. In his April 19, 1861, blockade proclamation, the president both claimed rights against the Confederates under the law of war, and declared his intent to refuse to recognize the rights of Confederate sailors under the same body of law. Along with the April 15 proclamation calling up the militia and the May draft response to the governor of Tennessee, the blockade proclamation illustrates the ambiguous, and even confused, policy of the Lincoln administration on the law governing its suppression of the rebellion at the beginning of the Civil War.

For several months, the administration continued to avoid deciding whether to apply the law of war in dealing with the rebellion, often leaving its generals in the field without guidance on how to deal with the enemy—as a belligerent army or as an armed criminal conspiracy. The administration was able to postpone taking a position on this issue in large part because of its decision to suspend the writ of habeas corpus.

On April 19, 1861, the Sixth Regiment of Massachusetts militia was attacked by a mob while passing through Baltimore, Maryland, on the way to Washington in response to the president's call. "At least 4 soldiers and 9 civilians were killed and many were injured"[22] in the melee. The governor of Maryland and the mayor of Baltimore called on the president to send no more troops through the city, and to reinforce the request the mayor and the police commissioner sent Baltimore police and local militia to burn railway bridges leading into Baltimore.[23] In partial response, on April 27 the president authorized Winfield Scott, the Commanding General of the Army, to suspend the writ of habeas corpus "at any point on or in the vicinity of any military line which is now or which shall be used between the city of Philadelphia and the city of Washington" if "you find resistance which renders it necessary." This authority could be exercised by General Scott either "personally or through the officer in command at the point where resistance occurs." On July 2, Scott's authority to suspend the writ was extended further north along the East Coast to New York City.[24]

In English and American law, the principal way to test whether there is a legal basis for someone's detention by the government is to apply to a court for a writ of habeas corpus. If the court accepts the application, it will issue the writ to the official holding the person in custody, ordering him to bring that person before the court and show the legal basis for the detention. The Constitution authorizes suspension of the "privilege of the Writ of Habeas Corpus" only "when in Cases of Rebellion or Invasion the public Safety may require it." The Constitution does not, however, say who—the president or Congress—has authority to suspend the writ in such cases. Chief Justice Taney, in a famous opinion, held that only Congress had this authority, and rejected the president's order of April 27 as unconstitutional.[25]

Among those acting on the order to burn railway bridges to Baltimore was Lieutenant John Merryman of the Baltimore County Horse Guards. On May 20, the U.S. military arrested Merryman for his actions and confined him in Fort McHenry. On May 26, Merryman applied to Chief Justice Taney for a writ of habeas corpus. The chief justice, who was at the time serving on a lower Federal court in Baltimore, ordered the commanding general of Fort McHenry to produce him and state the cause of his detention. Instead of producing the prisoner, General George Cadwalader wrote the chief justice a letter giving three reasons for his failure to appear with Merryman. First, he stated that Merryman was charged with "various acts of treason." This may have been a tactical mistake on Cadwalader's part, since treason was a Federal criminal offense clearly within the jurisdiction of the civilian courts, either Taney's court in Baltimore or another Federal court. The general then declared that Merryman was also charged with "being publicly associated with and holding a commission as lieutenant in a company having in their possession arms belonging to the United States, and avowing his purpose of armed hostility against the government," as well as his "readiness to cooperate with those engaged in the present rebellion against the United States." In other words, Merryman was an enemy combatant who held an official position in a military organization that had committed acts hostile to the United States. The general could simply have stated that Merryman was being held as a prisoner of war, but this would have implied that the law of war justified his detention. In May 1861, neither General Cadwalader nor anyone else knew whether the U.S. government would apply the law of war to the rebels. Finally, the general mentioned that he was "duly authorized by the President of the United States, in such cases, to suspend the writ of *habeas corpus,* for the public safety." He respectfully asked Taney's patience while he sought instructions from the president. Where the Lincoln administration was concerned, however, the chief justice had no patience.

Taney went through the farcical exercise of issuing an order for the arrest of General Cadwalader for contempt of court and sending a U.S. marshal to Fort McHenry to execute it. The marshal was of course turned away by armed sentries at the entrance to the fort. Taney then issued an opinion holding that only Congress, not the president, could suspend the writ, and calling on the president to execute the court's order. The opinion ignored Cadwalader's claim that the prisoner was, in effect, being held as a captured member of a hostile military unit during armed rebellion.

Just twelve years earlier, Chief Justice Taney had taken a somewhat different view of executive power in the face of a minor rebellion in Rhode Island. Then he had declared that the Federal courts should not question a government's decision to use military force to suppress an insurrection. "It was a state of war," he wrote approvingly, "and the established government resorted to the rights and usages of war to maintain itself, and to overcome the unlawful opposition." Applying the rights and usages of war, military officers serving the state government "might lawfully arrest anyone who, from the information before them, they had reasonable grounds to believe was engaged in the insurrection."[26] In 1861, however, Taney was not ready to accord President Lincoln the same deference he had given to the governor of Rhode Island in a much less serious insurrection.

Lincoln, in turn, ignored Taney's opinion and kept Merryman in custody. The president defended his suspension order in his July 4, 1861, message to the special session of Congress convened to deal with the Secession Crisis and ensuing rebellion, and promised that the attorney general would soon issue an opinion addressing the legal issues at more length.[27] Congress would eventually approve suspension of the writ, but not until 1863. In the meantime, the administration was faced with the problem of responding to Taney's conclusion that only Congress could suspend the writ. There was also the problem that suspension of the writ by itself did not give the Federal government the right to arrest persons without charge and to imprison them without trial. Suspension merely eliminated, for a time, the most effective way for those being held in custody to challenge the legality of their arrest and imprisonment. In theory, and often in practice, those aggrieved by illegal detention could later sue the officials who held them for false arrest and false imprisonment.[28]

For a solution to both problems, the administration turned to Attorney General Edward Bates. On July 5, 1861, one day after President Lincoln had promised it to the Congress, Attorney General Bates presented his written opinion on the habeas corpus issue.[29] The opinion responded to two questions from the president:

> First. In the present time of a great and dangerous insurrection has the President the discretionary power to cause to be arrested and held in custody persons known to have criminal intercourse with the insurgents or persons against whom there is probable cause for suspicion of such criminal complicity?

> Second. In such cases of arrest is the President justified in refusing to obey a writ of habeas corpus issued by a court or judge requiring him or his agent to produce the body of the prisoner and show the cause of his capture and detention to be adjudged and disposed of by such court or judge?

Neither question, it should be noted, asked about authority to suspend the writ, and Bates took the hint. Answering "yes" to both, he asserted that the executive had a positive right to detain certain persons in time of insurrection, based on the president's constitutional duty to suppress armed rebellion and the necessity of allowing him discretion to choose the means to do so:

[The President] is therefore necessarily thrown upon his discretion as to the manner in which he will use his means to meet the varying exigencies as they arise. If the insurgents assail the nation with an army he may find it best to meet them with an army and suppress the insurrection in the field of battle. If they seek to prolong the rebellion and gather strength by intercourse with foreign nations he may choose to guard the coasts and close the ports with a navy as one of the most efficient means to suppress the insurrection. And if they employ spies and emissaries to gather information, to forward secret supplies and to excite new insurrections in aid of the original rebellion he may find it both prudent and humane to arrest and imprison them. And this may be done either for the purpose of bringing them to trial and condign punishment for their crimes or they may be held in custody for the milder end of rendering them powerless for mischief until the exigency is past.

Turning to the president's second question, Bates hedged on whether the president or Congress could suspend the writ of habeas corpus. Rather, he advised that the president could ignore a writ issued in aid of persons held for actual or suspected "intercourse with the insurgents." To reach this conclusion it was not necessary, Bates declared, to decide who could suspend the writ:

For not doubting the power of the President to capture and hold by force insurgents in open arms against the Government and to arrest and imprison their suspected accomplices I never thought of first suspending the writ of habeas corpus any more than I thought of first suspending the writ of replevin[30] before seizing arms and munitions destined for the enemy.

The power to do these things is in the hand of the President, placed there by the Constitution and the statute law as a sacred trust to be used by him in his best discretion in the performance of his great first duty—to preserve, protect and defend the Constitution. And for any breach of that trust he is responsible before the high court of impeachment and before no other human tribunal.

In other words, when suppressing an insurrection, the president could ignore court orders to free someone like Merryman, just as he would ignore a court order to have the army attack Nashville and not Richmond. Both were operational decisions committed by the Constitution to the president, and the courts had no constitutional power to review them.

Attorney General Bates came very close to the reasoning of Justice Joseph Story that, as commander in chief, the president has, and must have, all powers necessary to win a war. He did not, however, take the extra logical step that Story did, and declare that these military powers are defined and limited by the international law of war.

The attorney general did find in the Constitution a presidential power to seize at least some property during an insurrection—"arms and munitions destined for the enemy," the very power that President Lincoln had asserted in his draft reply to the governor of Tennessee. So far, however, neither the president nor his chief lawyer were ready to resort to the law of war as the only source of limits on this power over private property. Opponents of emancipation would still have room to argue that the Constitution recognized the legitimacy of slavery, and that therefore that document cannot have given the president the power to interfere with it, even to suppress an insurrection.

The attorney general's work was soon put to use. On August 2, 1861, Commanding General Winfield Scott advised the commanding officer of the forts in New York harbor, where many political prisoners were sent, that "should the writ of habeas corpus come for the production in court of any of your political prisoners you will respond thereto that you deeply regret that pending existing political troubles you cannot comply with the requisition of the honorable judge."[31] Similar instructions were sent to other army posts holding political prisoners.

Under these orders, suspension of the writ was not even to be mentioned as a ground for refusing to obey a court. This defense was to be held in reserve and used only when the government took action against persons not covered by the attorney general's opinion. Strictly speaking, that opinion applied only to "insurgents in open arms against the Government" and "their suspected accomplices." Although Bates did not refer to the law of nations in his opinion, these were precisely the type of prisoners whose detention was authorized by the law of war.

The Lincoln administration held relatively few persons whose confinement was not authorized by the law of war because of their direct involvement in preparing and conducting armed hostilities against the government, or because they were enemy "nationals"—citizens of the Confederacy.[32] However, some of the political prisoners taken in 1861 were held for reasons that could not be justified under even the most expansive interpretation of the president's war powers as limited by the law of war. These cases provide some of the strongest evidence against the Lincoln administration on the charge of abusing civil liberties. As a means of keeping military communications open between Washington, D.C., and the loyal states to its north after rioters had attacked Massachusetts troops moving through Baltimore, the president authorized suspension of the writ along the East Coast of the United States. The suspension was eventually extended as far along the coast as Boston, but elsewhere Federal and state courts still had the power to issue writs of habeas corpus. Prime examples of abuse were to be found among the cases of prisoners who were arrested in a part of the country where the writ of habeas corpus was still authorized, but who were then moved to an area where it had been suspended because the government had no firm legal ground for holding them.

In British and American law, the writ of habeas corpus can only be issued by a court with jurisdiction over an official who actually has a detained person in custody. In 1861, Lieutenant John Merryman, for example, was being held at Fort McHenry in Baltimore harbor. He could only apply for a writ of habeas corpus to the U.S. Circuit Court having jurisdiction over the territory where he was being held (Maryland). Federal courts located in other jurisdictions, such as Pennsylvania or Delaware, would have refused his application on the ground that they had no jurisdiction over the official holding him, the commanding officer of Fort McHenry.

Suspension of the writ in 1861, supplemented by the attorney general's July 2 opinion, allowed the government to delay or avoid choosing a legal basis for holding people taken into custody for reasons related to the rebellion. At least for a time, prisoners of war, spies, and guerrillas could be intermingled with criminal suspects, and all could be held as "political prisoners" without their exact status being defined. The administration's persistent reluctance to distinguish criminal suspects, political prisoners, and prisoners of war is most clearly illustrated by its reliance on U.S. marshals, rather than the military, to deal with persons aiding the Confederacy and other cases of alleged disloyalty.

On the Atlantic coast, where the situation was most directly under the supervision of Washington, marshals took the lead in dealing with persons aiding the Confederacy, and other supposed threats to internal security. When the mayor of Newport wrote to Secretary William H. Seward that he had "good reason to believe that there are several disloyal persons in this city . . . who have been and are in communication with the rebels in various secret ways," and asked what steps he should take to cause their arrest, he was referred to the U.S. marshal for the District of Rhode Island.[33] In Boston, Seward directed the U.S. marshal to "take effective measures to break up the business of making and sending shoes for the rebel army or other articles for like purposes," and authorized the employment of two detectives for this purpose.[34] In New York City, the military garrison was directed to help the local U.S. marshal make arrests, rather than the other way around.[35] On the other hand, it was the "marshals of the United States in the vicinity of forts where political prisoners are held," rather than the army, who were given responsibility for providing "decent lodging and subsistence for such prisoners."[36]

On at least one occasion, a U.S. marshal took the initiative to suppress what he regarded as a disloyal activity, with results that embarrassed the Lincoln administration. On September 3, 1861, Marshal David H. Carr of Connecticut telegraphed Secretary of War Simon Cameron that, to "prevent a greater calamity," he had "taken it upon [himself] to interdict and entirely prohibit the sale and circulation of the New York Daily News in the city of New Haven, it being quite evident to me that our citizens as a body do not desire its circulation nor will they longer allow it." It is not clear why Marshal Carr requested Cameron's approval, since Secretary of State Seward usually dealt with U.S. marshals on internal security matters. Nevertheless, Cameron immediately telegraphed his approval of the marshal's actions, a decision that itself suggests why Seward, rather than Cameron, had been given responsibility for these issues.[37] The secretary of war does not seem to have considered why, if the New York Daily News threatened to cause a "calamity" if circulated in Connecticut, the Federal authorities in New York City had not also seen it as a threat. (Two weeks later, the superintendent of police in New York reported to Secretary Seward that the pro-secessionist editorial policy of the Daily News was becoming less evident—"more and more insipid"—every day.)[38]

On September 11, Marshal Carr reported to Cameron that his order was being defied by "a noisy secessionist" named George A. Hubbell, who continued to sell the Daily News on trains of the Naugatuck

Railroad. Reluctant to go too far on his own responsibility, Carr asked for an order "from yourself or Mr. Seward" to arrest Hubbell.[39] Cameron again complied. George Hubbell was arrested on September 20 and sent to Fort Lafayette in New York harbor.[40] Fortunately for him, his brother, a Methodist minister active in the New York Republican Party, intervened with President Lincoln. According to his brother, Hubbell, "a cripple from his youth with a spinal deformity," had only spoken out in anger about Marshal Carr's interference with his business. The president of the railroad, rather than the newsboy, decided what papers should be sold on the trains.[41] Seward ordered Hubbell's release five days later.

Without policy guidance from the administration, generals in the field were unsure whether their soldiers were primarily fighting a war or enforcing state and Federal law. The guidance that was provided was of little practical use. On November 12, General George B. McClellan gave the commanding general of the Department of the Ohio unhelpful advice to "religiously respect the constitutional rights of all," but only as "far as military necessity will permit."[42]

In 1864, General William Tecumseh Sherman would press the law of war to its limits in his treatment of enemy civilians and civilian property. In November 1861, however, his orders implied that law enforcement was the primary function of his army in Kentucky. "When prisoners are received have the papers all handed to Judge Bullitt, a good Union man and a member of the court of appeals, to whose decision I leave the case," he wrote to one of his subordinates. "We cannot imprison and keep in custody all suspected persons, and the only safe course is to follow the law of the State of Kentucky which makes arrests only proper when overt acts of treason are established." The preferred way to handle rebels was not to send them to camps in the North as prisoners of war, but rather to have them post bonds to guarantee future good behavior. For this purpose, General Sherman asked the local Federal judge to appoint a number of commissioners in the Department of the Cumberland: "Judge Catron says the commissioners can put them under bond and the bond will be good against their property or the property of their sureties. As you can well understand we would soon fill all the places of confinement in Louisville were we to arrest and imprison all who may be dangerous. Leaders and conspicuous men never should be arrested unless in strong cases, and then an examination should be had before a commissioner of the United States."[43] His purpose, Sherman declared, was to prevent cruelties that "would not be tolerated by the laws of war or peace," a choice of words that reveals his own uncertainty about which set of rules applied to the operations of his army.

Brigadier General Don Carlos Buell, commanding the Department of the Ohio in the fall of 1861, also initially assumed that rebels and disloyal persons detained by his forces would be tried in the Federal courts for violations of civilian criminal law. On December 5, 1861, he therefore asked army headquarters for help in prosecuting the large number of persons his command had detained. Since the U.S. district attorney did not reside near Buell's headquarters at Louisville, Kentucky, he asked that an assistant district attorney be appointed to prosecute the more serious cases of aiding the enemy.[44] The War Department naturally referred the request to the attorney general, who on December 30 informed Buell that the government had no plans to prosecute anyone in the general's custody. Aiding the enemy was not at that time an offense in Federal criminal law, so Attorney General Bates said there was little he could do to help General Buell. Nor could Bates advise the general on what he should do with these people, aside from continuing to hold them as political prisoners, in a state of legal limbo:

> I do not wonder that General Buell is put to difficulty about "the disposition of prisoners accused of giving aid to the enemy." I share in that difficulty, and mainly because in these disordered times it is hard to draw the exact line of separation between the different kinds of arrests as distinguished by their different purposes and objects—that is judicial arrest whose only object is to secure the presence of the accused so that he may be tried for an alleged crime before a civil court, and political arrest—which is usually executed by the military arm—whose object is to secure the prisoner and hold him subject to the somewhat broad and as yet undefined discretion of the President as political chief of the nation. As to arrests merely political or military they are as I understand the law beyond the reach of the judicial officers and subject only to the political power of the President, who may at his discretion dispose of the prisoners by orders addressed to his subordinate officers either civil or military. Without such order

I have no authority to give any direction touching the disposition of political or military prisoners.[45]

By the end of August 1861, the geographic scale of the conflict from the Mississippi to the Atlantic, and the size and organization of the opposing forces, made it more and more difficult for the Lincoln administration to ignore the fact that it was engaged in a full-scale war. Increasingly, commanders in the field and the government in Washington found that problems raised by waging war could be dealt with more effectively by applying the law of war rather than trying to maintain the tattered fiction that their armies were just enforcing Federal law. The Civil War was not the Whiskey Rebellion.

4

The Union Applies
the Law of War

Not until April 1863 did the Federal government issue a formal statement declaring its intention to apply the law of war to Confederate
forces. Long before then, however, that law had been applied in practice
by both the Union and Confederate armies. The Lincoln administration accepted the law of war little by little, in response to specific needs
and pressures during the first year of the Civil War. At each stage, the
process was gradual and hesitant out of concern that allowing yet another rule of international law to govern relations with the rebels would
accord too much official recognition to what the president termed "the
so-called Confederate States of America."

The initial step in this process was to treat captured Confederate
soldiers as prisoners of war rather than accused criminals or political
prisoners. Prisoner of war treatment was soon followed by informal exchanges of prisoners between Confederate and U.S. armed forces. At
about the same time, the government reluctantly accepted the necessity
of allowing military-to-military communications under a flag of truce.
Soon the U.S. Army began to use military commissions to enforce the
law of war against unlawful belligerents and spies. Eventually, in early
1862, the administration authorized the negotiation of a formal agreement for the exchange of prisoners of war on a regular basis. Only then,
when the Confederacy was enjoying all the rights of an enemy under
the law of war, did the United States consider applying the full rigor of
this law to enemy private property, including property in slaves. It was
out of this decision that the Emancipation Proclamation grew.

Several factors pushed the Lincoln administration to grant captured
Confederate soldiers the status of prisoners of war. To begin with, there
was the simple force of bureaucratic inertia within the U.S. Army. Army

regulations told officers how to treat prisoners of war; they said nothing about how to handle criminal suspects or political prisoners. Without orders to the contrary from the War Department, middle-rank army officers were inclined to apply the regulations on prisoners of war to any enemy personnel in their custody. As early as June 1861, for example, staff officers in Missouri and Virginia were referring to captives as "prisoners of war" in official correspondence.[1]

A more direct source of pressure came from generals and civilian officials who required instruction on how to deal with the rebels and other "political prisoners" they had in custody. The event that first forced the administration to apply the law of war to Confederate soldiers was General George McClellan's July campaign to take control of the pro-Union counties in western Virginia. On June 28, as he prepared for the campaign, McClellan asked Commanding General Winfield Scott for guidance on the treatment of prisoners: "I beg leave to ask for instructions as to what disposition is to be made of prisoners of the following classes respectively: First. Prisoners taken in battle. Second. Prisoners who have been in the secession army and have deserted or been discharged. Third. Spies. Fourth. Guerrillas. Fifth. Prisoners who without taking up arms themselves have been active and influential in inducing others to take up arms."[2] This request went unanswered.

The success of the West Virginia campaign finally forced the government to adopt a prisoner of war policy. On July 13, Lieutenant Colonel John Pegram of the Confederate army surrendered himself and more than 500 of his men to McClellan's forces. McClellan telegraphed army headquarters that he had agreed "to treat them with the kindness due prisoners of war, but stating that it was not in my power to relieve them from any liability incurred by taking arms against the United States." McClellan, sensitive to the political nuances of the surrender terms, never promised Colonel Pegram that his men would *be* prisoners of war, only that they would be given the same standard of treatment (subject, of course, to the possibility of being tried for treason). When Pegram's men were added to prisoners already taken, McClellan would have almost 1,000 people in custody, and he asked army headquarters for "immediate instructions by telegraph as to the disposition to be made of officers and men taken prisoners of war."[3] The prisoner of war issue was no longer theoretical.

Fortunately, McClellan's earlier dispatch on June 28 seems to have led the Washington bureaucracy to begin serious consideration of the issue. On July 12, the army quartermaster general, Montgomery Meigs, had advised the secretary of war that the army should start to plan for the reception and treatment of prisoners of war. He also gave Secretary Simon Cameron a short tutorial on the mechanics of handling prisoners according to the laws and customs of war: "Prisoners of war are entitled to proper accommodations, to courteous and respectful treatment, to one ration a day and to consideration according to rank. Heretofore when the Government has had prisoners to care for a commissary of prisoners has been appointed." Moreover, the officer selected to be commissary of prisoners should possess certain qualifications of character, rank, and experience: "The provost-marshal is the chief superintending keeper of prisoners, but in rank and position the commissary of prisoners is much higher than the provost-marshal. Large sums of money may pass through the hands of the commissary of prisoners. The negotiation of exchange of prisoners is important. A lieutenant-colonel has been exchanged for a captain and ten privates; a general for a certain number of other officers. Knowledge of military law and custom is needed in order not to offend by errors of ignorance in treating these delicate questions."[4] Meigs, an experienced regular officer, would have written such a letter only if his superiors had asked for it. His advice to proceed carefully in selecting a commissary of prisoners was apparently heeded, since Lieutenant Colonel William Hoffman was not detailed for that duty until late October.[5]

In the meantime, the War Department was able to respond quickly to General McClellan's July 13 telegram. The next day, General Scott wired unambiguous instructions that these Confederate soldiers would be regarded as prisoners of war, with the privilege of being paroled:

Discharge all your prisoners of war under the grade of commissioned officers who shall willingly take and subscribe a general oath in these terms:

"I swear (or affirm) that I will not take up arms against the United States or serve in any military capacity whatsoever against them until regularly discharged according to the usages of war from this obligation."

As to officers among your prisoners permit all to return to their homes who willingly sign a written general parole in these words:

"We and each of us for himself severally pledge our words

of honor as officers and gentlemen that we will not again take up arms against the United States nor serve in any military capacity whatsoever against them until regularly discharged according to the usages of war from this obligation."[6]

It is curious that, in the egalitarian culture of nineteenth-century America, these instructions would try to preserve the aristocratic distinction between commissioned officers, who were gentlemen, and enlisted men, who were not. The former could pledge their word of honor, while the latter, who presumably had no sense of honor, were asked to take an oath. Perhaps General Scott, known to the army as "Old Fuss and Feathers," had insisted on retaining this formal distinction. It died out after he retired in the fall of 1861.

The "usages of war" was another name for the laws of war, and the inclusion of this term in the oath and parole made it clear that, at least for now, the U.S. government would deal with these men under international law and not the domestic law of treason. The reference to being "regularly discharged" from their oath or parole implied that the government contemplated the possibility of exchanging prisoners with the Confederate forces.

Although General Scott's telegram provided for the parole of enemy soldiers taken in battle, it gave McClellan no guidance on how to deal with the other categories of prisoners he mentioned in his June 28 telegram—spies, guerrillas, and civilian Confederate sympathizers. In 1861, Federal civilian courts had no jurisdiction over espionage cases. Under the law of war, spies and guerrillas could be tried by military commission and sentenced to death or imprisonment, but the government was not yet ready to go that far. Instead, the captives who had not been paroled as prisoners of war were sent to the rear and confined at Camp Chase, Ohio. On August 7, the governor of Ohio asked the secretary of war what should be done with them. Receiving no reply, he wrote again a week later, but received no answer to that letter either.[7] Those who were not prisoners of war would still be held in limbo as political prisoners.

Meanwhile, the decision to regard Confederate soldiers as prisoners of war began to have an impact outside the western Virginia theater of war. In its official communications, army headquarters started to distinguish prisoners of war from political prisoners in military custody. On July 19, General Scott ordered the new commanding officer of Forts

Hamilton and Lafayette, New York, to keep "an exact account" of the costs of maintaining his prisoners of war, undoubtedly so that the U.S. government could demand reimbursement in any future peace negotiations with the rebels.[8] Similar orders were later given to the commanding officer of Fort Warren, in Boston harbor, when that post prepared to receive an overflow of prisoners from New York. In addition, the commander of Fort Warren was told that, "should writs of habeas corpus be served on you for the prisoners of war you will respond thereto that they are held as prisoners of war, and in these cases and also in any case of a political prisoner you will reply you deeply regret that pending existing political troubles you cannot comply with the requisition of the honorable judge." Finally, in November Secretary Seward directed that prisoners of war be separated from political prisoners and confined at a different location.[9]

As a matter of practical politics, the decision to grant prisoner of war status to Confederate soldiers became irrevocable after the First Battle of Bull Run on July 21, when the Confederate army captured more than 1,400 Union prisoners. Most of these were citizen-soldiers, militiamen who had been called into Federal service under the president's April proclamation. During their enforced stay in Richmond they did not hesitate to complain to their representatives in Congress about prison conditions and the failure of the administration to obtain their exchange or release on parole. Their representatives in Congress made sure that this message was received at the War Department. The administration now had to face the political problem of securing adequate care and humane treatment for its own prisoners of war in the hands of the Confederate government. Any further temptation to treat Confederate soldiers and sailors as accused criminals would produce retaliation in kind.

This lesson was driven home when the administration tried to deny prisoner of war status to Confederate seamen who were caught attacking Northern merchant shipping. President Lincoln's April 19 proclamation declaring a blockade of Confederate ports had threatened that, "if any person under the pretended authority of the said [Confederate] States . . . shall molest a vessel of the United States, or the persons or cargo on board of her, such persons will be held amenable to the laws of the United States for the prevention and punishment of piracy."[10] On June 5, 1861, the U.S. Navy squadron blockading Charleston, South Carolina, captured the Confederate privateer *Savannah*, manned by a crew of three officers and ten sailors. In accordance with the president's proclamation, the flag officer in command declared the *Savannah* to be "a piratical schooner,"[11] and sent the ship and the prisoners to New York City for legal proceedings. Although the thirteen crewmen were not immediately brought to trial, they were held in jail on charges of piracy and treason. In response, Jefferson Davis warned President Lincoln that "this Government will deal out to the prisoners held by it the same treatment and the same fate as shall be experienced by those captured in the *Savannah;* and if driven to the terrible necessity of retaliation by your execution of any of the officers or crew of the Savannah that retaliation will be extended so far as shall be requisite to secure the abandonment by you of a practice unknown to the warfare of civilized man and so barbarous as to disgrace the nation which shall be guilty of inaugurating it."[12]

On July 6, while the crew of the *Savannah* were awaiting trial in New York, the Confederate privateer *Jeff Davis* captured the Boston schooner *Enchantress.* The Confederate prize crew, under the command of Lieutenant William Smith, was placed aboard the *Enchantress* to sail her back to Charleston, the home port of the *Jeff Davis.* With one ominous exception, the civilian crew of the *Enchantress* were taken aboard the *Jeff Davis* to be held as prisoners of war. The exception was the ship's cook, a free African American named James Garrick. Lieutenant Smith was overheard to remark that the cook would "fetch $1,500 when we get him into Charleston."[13] Garrick would be sold into slavery if the *Enchantress* made it to South Carolina.

Fortunately for him, the voyage to Charleston was interrupted on July 22 when the *Enchantress* was stopped off Cape Hatteras by the U.S. warship *Albatross.* Lieutenant Smith and his prize crew tried to bluff their way out of the situation by pretending to be the original Boston crew of the *Enchantress,* but James Garrick, perhaps sensing that this was his last chance to remain a free man, jumped overboard and swam toward the warship, calling out that the *Enchantress* had been captured by Confederates. Lieutenant Smith and the prize crew were brought to Philadelphia as prisoners of the U.S. Navy, where they too were charged with piracy.

The U.S. district attorney for the Eastern District of Pennsylvania moved with more dispatch than his colleague in New York, and William Smith was brought to trial in Philadelphia on October 22, 1861. Convicted after a one-day trial, he was sentenced to hang as a pirate.

When word of this conviction was received in Richmond, Jefferson Davis acted to carry out his threat of retaliation, using the prisoners captured at Bull Run. On November 10, lots were drawn under the supervision of the Confederate provost-marshal of Richmond to select fourteen Federal officers to be held hostage for Lieutenant Smith and the thirteen *Savannah* crewmen. The adjutant general of the U.S. Army was notified "that the punishment of the officers held as hostages would be precisely the same as that of the prisoners on trial or tried in Philadelphia and New York."[14]

Ultimately, the Lincoln administration found itself powerless to deal with this situation short of complete capitulation. Six of the hostages were colonels of militia regiments from New York, Massachusetts, and Kentucky. These were influential men in the politics of their respective states, and the administration could not simply allow them to be hanged or imprisoned as felons. In January 1862, the U.S. government tried to exchange Colonel Pegram for one of the hostages. The offer was refused. Only if "the privateersmen are put on the same footing as the other prisoners of war" would the Confederates "then release such officers as are now retained as hostages."[15]

Next, the government offered to exchange Lieutenant Smith, then being held under sentence of death as a convicted pirate, for Colonel Michael Corcoran of the 69th New York Militia Regiment, whom the Confederate authorities had designated as being specifically held as a hostage for Smith. This offer, too, was refused. The Confederate officer in charge of the negotiations made it clear that his government would "not take into consideration any proposition for exchange of our privateers taken in our service on the high seas until there is an absolute, unconditional abandonment of the pretext that they are pirates, and until they are released from the position of felons and placed in the same condition as other prisoners of war, and we decline receiving any proposal in relation to the hostages who we are forced unwillingly to treat as felons as long as our fellow-citizens are so treated by the enemy."[16]

The Lincoln administration capitulated on January 31, 1862. Secretary of State Seward ordered the U.S. marshals in Philadelphia and New York to transfer Lieutenant Smith and the other privateers to the custody of the army, which would hold them as prisoners of war. Ten days later, the Confederate government was notified of this order.[17]

By the time the hostage incident was resolved, the U.S. government had reluctantly granted the Confederate government virtually all the privileges accorded to belligerent powers under the laws of war. From the very beginning of the conflict, Federal officers in the field had communicated with their Confederate counterparts under flags of truce, ostensibly without the knowledge or authorization of their superiors in the national capital. By the end of July 1861, the passage of a flag-of-truce boat between the generals commanding Fortress Monroe and the Confederate port of Norfolk, Virginia, had become routine.

The need for quasi-official communications under a flag of truce seems to have been initially accepted by the Lincoln administration in mid-August 1861. As of August 2, Secretary of State Seward had no official channel to ask the Confederate authorities whether Congressman Alfred Ely of New York had been killed or taken prisoner at Bull Run; instead, he relied on a private telegram to confirm the congressman's capture. By August 22, however, Secretary of War Cameron did not hesitate to direct that twenty-three paroled Confederate prisoners be returned to the South on the flag-of-truce boat running between Norfolk and Fortress Monroe.[18]

The decision to seek formal negotiation of a prisoner exchange cartel, in accordance with the laws of war, was the most difficult for the Lincoln administration to accept. As late as December 10, 1861, Attorney General Edward Bates objected to regular prisoner exchanges as granting too much recognition to the Confederacy.[19] Bates's concerns were shared by politically sensitive Union officers in the field. In October, Ulysses S. Grant, then an obscure general in the Western theater of war, informed Confederate general Leonidas Polk that, "in regard to the exchange of prisoners proposed I can of my own accord make none. I recognize no Southern Confederacy myself but will communicate with higher authority for their views."[20] Another Federal general replied to a similar request in more detail: "I am in receipt of your communication dated on the 24th instant requesting an exchange of prisoners. To do this would imply that the Government of the United States admits the existing civil war to be between independent nations. This I cannot admit and must therefore decline to make any terms or conditions in reference to those we mutually hold as prisoners taken in arms without the orders of my Government."[21]

Tortuous subterfuges were adopted to avoid the appearance of negotiating with the rebels. A paroled Confederate prisoner might be sent back through his own lines to arrange the release of a Union prisoner of equal rank, after which he would be formally released from the terms of his parole.[22] Another common fiction was to arrange for parallel "humanitarian" releases of a certain number of prisoners by each side.[23] It was, of course, in the Confederacy's interest to avoid subterfuge and insist on formal prisoner exchanges, and to institutionalize the exchanges in a formal cartel between the two sides. The hostage crisis arising from Lieutenant Smith's piracy conviction allowed the Confederate government to increase the pressure toward both goals.

The hostage crisis, together with uncertainty about the fate of Union prisoners taken at Bull Run and later Confederate victories, also led to increased pressure for exchanges from the North. State governors and influential private citizens urged Lincoln to negotiate an exchange of prisoners.[24] On December 11, 1861, the House of Representatives passed a resolution requesting the president "to inaugurate systematic measures for the exchange of prisoners in the present rebellion."[25]

In January 1862, the Confederate authorities tried to initiate negotiations for a formal prisoner exchange cartel through the channel of communications between Norfolk and Fortress Monroe. On January 20, General Benjamin Huger, commanding the garrison at Norfolk, wrote to his Union counterpart that the Confederate government was "willing and anxious to exchange prisoners on fair terms, and as the authorities at Washington have permitted it in certain cases I beg your assistance in making it general and thus aid the cause of humanity and civilization."[26] Noting that the letter was "worthy of consideration," General John Wool forwarded it to army headquarters: "As the exchange of prisoners is now established would it not save you and myself a great deal of labor and trouble if the two Governments appointed agents to attend to it? It could be done with more system and regularity, and the officers and men might be kept together."[27] The Lincoln administration capitulated on this issue as well. On February 11, Edwin M. Stanton, the new secretary of war, directed the commanding general at Fortress Monroe to begin cartel negotiations with his counterpart at Norfolk:

> You will inform General Huger that you alone are clothed with full powers for the purpose of arranging for exchange of prisoners. . . . You may arrange for the restoration of all the prisoners to their homes on fair terms of exchange, man for man and officer for officer of equal grade, assimilating the grade of officers of the Army and Navy when necessary, and agreeing upon equitable terms for the number of men or officers of inferior

grade to be exchanged for any of higher grade when the occasion shall arise. That all the surplus prisoners on either side to be discharged on parole, with the agreement that any prisoners of war taken by the other party shall be returned in exchange as fast as captured, and this system to be continued while hostilities continue so that on all occasions either party holding prisoners shall so hold them only on parole till exchanged, the prisoners being allowed to remain in their own region till the exchange is effected.[28]

The initial negotiations did not go well. On February 23, representatives of the two sides met and exchanged drafts for an exchange cartel. The Confederate draft agreement included a provision that the capturing party would transport paroled or exchanged prisoners to the "frontier of their own country free of expense to the prisoners and at the expense of the capturing party." This phrase was politically loaded, since it implied that the United States and the Confederacy were two different countries. General Wool sensed that there was something wrong with this provision from the Union point of view, but could not quite put his finger on it. He therefore objected to it for reasons of cost and requested further instructions from Washington.[29] The secretary of war saw the proposal as evidence of Confederate bad faith and told Wool to break off negotiations: "The proposition is obnoxious in its terms and import and wholly inadmissible, and as the terms you were authorized to offer have not been accepted you will make no arrangement at present except for actual exchanges."[30]

Confederate commissioner Howell Cobb then offered to change the language to provide for the return of prisoners to the "frontier of the line of hostilities,"[31] a politically neutral phrase. By this time, so much suspicion had been aroused on the Union side that the negotiations dragged on for months, and an exchange cartel was not signed until July 22, 1862. By even entering into these negotiations, however, the Lincoln administration was conceding that Confederate soldiers and sailors would be prisoners of war, treated in accordance with the international laws of war, at least as long as the conflict continued.

5

The Law as a Weapon

During the fall and winter of 1861–1862, while the U.S. government slowly conceded to Confederate forces the rights of international belligerents, U.S. military commanders in the field started to use the law of war as a sword against the rebels. The president had begun this process himself in April when he claimed the right to prohibit neutral trade with Southern seaports by placing them under a blockade. In the fall, Federal authorities increasingly claimed the right to punish, as unlawful combatants, guerrillas and bushwhackers who attacked Union forces and military assets behind U.S. military lines without being enrolled in any unit recognized by the Confederate military or while wearing civilian clothing rather than Confederate uniforms.

General John C. Frémont, commanding Federal forces west of the Mississippi from his headquarters in St. Louis, was first to threaten Confederate guerrillas with punishment under the laws of war. During the Mexican War, Frémont, then a major in the Army Topographical Engineers, had participated in the American conquest of California, and he had lived there for a time after leaving the army. He therefore had some familiarity with the practice of using military courts to govern occupied territory and suppress attacks from unlawful combatants. In Missouri, Frémont believed he faced problems similar to those the U.S. Army had encountered in territories conquered from Mexico.

In 1861, the population of Missouri was divided in its loyalties. Pro-Union Missouri volunteers were raised by Nathaniel Lyon, a U.S. Army officer, while pro-Confederate officials organized the Missouri State Guards under the command of Sterling Price. In the middle of June, Federal forces advanced from St. Louis to the state capital at Jefferson City, forcing General Price's army to retreat to the southwestern part of the state. Some members of the State Guard remained behind and, with Price's encouragement, began to burn railroad bridges, destroy telegraph lines, and engage in other acts of guerrilla war against the Federal forces.

After General Frémont took command of the Department of the West on July 25, he realized that much of Missouri was in effect occupied hostile territory, just as California had been in 1846, and that the laws of war could be applied to the local population to discourage guerrilla activities. Frémont may have gotten this idea from one of his subordinates, General John Pope. In response to sniper attacks on Union troop trains near Palmyra, Missouri, Pope had ordered one of his subordinates to "have the men who did the firing . . . tried by a military commission which you will order and at once execute the sentence of the commission upon them."[1] Unfortunately, General Pope was not a legal expert, and the officer to whom this order was directed did not have the authority to convene military commissions. Any trials he ordered would be illegal.

On August 30, General Frémont issued a public proclamation announcing his intention to adopt Pope's policies in dealing with guerrillas.

> The lines of the army occupation in this State are for the present declared to extend from Leavenworth by way of posts of Jefferson City, Rolla and Ironton to Cape Girardeau on the Mississippi River. All persons who shall be taken with arms in their hands within these lines shall be tried by court-martial and if found guilty will be shot. Real and personal property of those who shall take up arms against the United States or who shall be directly proven to have taken an active part with their enemies in the field is declared confiscated to public use and their slaves if any they have are hereby declared free men.[2]

According to a biographer sympathetic to Frémont, the proclamation was drafted quickly, with his "accustomed impetuosity,"[3] and much of its language was overbroad or inappropriate. The wording of the proclamation was so imprecise that it appeared to apply to regular Confederate soldiers captured in uniform and in open battle. One of General Frémont's subordinates even asked whether the proclamation required him to shoot enemy wounded captured on a field of battle, leaving a horrified Frémont to reply that he wanted it "clearly understood that the proclamation is intended distinctly to recognize all the usual rights of an open enemy in the field and to be in all respects strictly conformable to the ordinary usages of war."[4]

Another indication of haste was the threat to send illegal combatants before a "court-martial"—Frémont was actually referring to trial by a military commission. Unfortunately, Frémont's implementation of the proclamation was no improvement over its drafting, and he failed to efficiently supervise the military commission trials held under his regime. The errors initiated by General Pope continued, and many of the trials turned out to be legally defective.[5] These errors were not corrected until General Henry Halleck, a noted expert on the laws of war, took command in the West late in 1861.

The most serious and immediate controversy concerning Frémont's proclamation centered not on military commissions, but on its declaration that the "property of those who shall take up arms against the United States . . . is declared confiscated to public use and their slaves . . . are hereby declared free men."[6] Almost immediately, prominent citizens of Kentucky wrote the president to oppose Frémont's action.[7] With a pro-Confederate governor and a pro-Union legislature, in the fall of 1861 Kentucky was still officially neutral in the Civil War. Both Confederate and U.S. forces hovered near its borders, waiting to see which way the state would fall. In this sensitive situation, Frémont's emancipation proclamation had an immediate, adverse impact on public opinion, and Kentucky's pro-slavery population began to lean toward secession. Lincoln's political allies in Kentucky frantically wrote to the president that he must rescind the emancipation provisions of Frémont's proclamation or lose Kentucky to the Confederates. After an unsuccessful effort to persuade General Frémont to modify the proclamation himself, President Lincoln peremptorily ordered him to change it to conform to the confiscation act Congress had passed in August.[8]

Less than a week after the president modified Frémont's proclamation, Senator Orville Hickman Browning wrote Lincoln to protest that decision. Browning's friendship with Lincoln went back to the late 1830s, when both had been members of the Whig party in the Illinois state legislature. Later they both worked to found the Illinois Republican Party, and most recently Browning had joined Lincoln in Washington after having been appointed to fill the Senate seat vacated by the death of Stephen A. Douglas.[9]

With Congress adjourned, Browning was back in Quincy, Illinois, where on September 17 he wrote the president that it had been a political mistake to alter Frémont's emancipation policy. "That proclamation had the unqualified approval of every true friend of the Government within my knowledge. . . . Its influence was most salutary, and it was accomplishing much good. Its revocation disheartens our friends, and represses their ardor." It was true, Browning admitted, that there was "no express, written law authorizing it"; but, he countered, "war is never carried on, and can never be, in strict accordance with previously adjusted constitutional and legal provisions."[10]

President Lincoln shot back a reply on September 22, expressing astonishment at his friend's position. Browning and Lincoln were both lawyers, and the president's letter focused on the hard, technical issues of property law raised by a military emancipation proclamation:

> Genl Fremont's proclamation, as to confiscation of property, and the liberation of slaves, is *purely political*, and not within the range of *military* law, or necessity. If a commanding General finds a necessity to seize the farm of a private owner, for a pasture, an encampment, or a fortification, he has the right to do so, and to so hold it, as long as the necessity lasts; and this is within military law, because within military necessity—But to say the farm shall no longer belong to the owner, or his heirs forever; and this as well when the farm is *not* needed for military purposes, as when it is, is purely political, without the savor of military law about it—And the same is true of slaves—If the General needs them, he can seize them and use them; but when the need is past, it is not for him to fix their permanent future condition—That must be settled according to laws made by law-makers, and not by military proclamations—The proclamation, in the point in question, is simply "dictatorship."

"Can it be pretended that it is any longer the government" of the United States, the president asked, or "any government of constitution & laws,—wherein a General, or a President may make permanent rules of property by proclamation[?] . . . What I object to, is that I, as President, shall expressly, or impliedly, seize and exercise the permanent legislative functions of the government. . . ."[11]

Historians have generally taken this letter at face value as a sincere and accurate statement of Lincoln's views on emancipation as of the time it was written. David Herbert Donald, for example, characterized the letter as a "carefully reasoned defense" by the president of his actions against Frémont. Browning's objections were, Donald concluded, "the last thing [Lincoln] expected from a man who prided himself on his conservatism and his adhesion to the letter of the Constitution."[12] Allen Guelzo, in his recent study of the Emancipation Proclamation, wrote that the letter "bristled with irritation but contained Lincoln's most sustained exposition of what the Constitution and the war permitted him, as president, to do."[13]

The chief problem with the traditional interpretation of Lincoln's September 22 letter is that ten months later, on July 22, 1862, he told his cabinet that he had decided to issue an emancipation proclamation of his own, based on his powers as commander in chief of the army and navy. He followed through on this decision and issued a preliminary emancipation proclamation on September 22, 1862, exactly one year after suggesting to Orville Browning that as president he had no military authority to free any slaves. In light of what followed in less than a year, the traditional interpretation of the letter to Browning allows critics to argue that Lincoln's Emancipation Proclamation was at best an act of hypocrisy and at worst a willful violation of the Constitution as he understood it.

It is more likely that the September 22 letter was not written to convince Browning that Lincoln had been right in his handling of General Frémont. Rather, it was sent to goad Browning into framing the best arguments he could in favor of the constitutionality of an emancipation proclamation. Several of Lincoln's contemporaries noted his fondness for arguing against the very position he wanted to support, particularly where emancipation was an issue. John Hay recalled that during the summer of 1862, while Lincoln was considering an emancipation proclamation, "if any one tried to dissuade him from it, he gave the argument in its favor. If others urged it upon him, he exhausted the reasoning against it."[14] One of his earliest biographers called attention to "Mr. Lincoln's peculiarity of arguing against his own conclusions" and attributed it to "the old practice of his legal career, of arguing his opponent's side of the question—often for the simple purpose, evidently, of winning support for his own convictions."[15]

There are reasons to think that the September 22 letter to Browning was an early example of this practice. In his annual message for 1863, President Lincoln told Congress that he had known he might have to use emancipation as a weapon since early in the war: "For a long time it had been hoped that the rebellion could be suppressed without resorting to it as a military measure. It was all the while deemed possible that the necessity for it might come. . . ."[16] If that were true, then it is very plausible that Lincoln would have been collecting legal arguments in favor of emancipation as early as September 1861.

It is hard to take too seriously Lincoln's declaration that Browning's position "astonished" him. Orville H. Browning had been among the very first, along with Senator Charles Sumner, to urge the president to issue an emancipation proclamation. At the end of April 1861, Browning wrote a long, rambling letter to the president, offering advice on the future course of the war. Toward the end, he predicted that "the time is not yet, but it will come when it will be necessary for you to march an army into the South, and proclaim freedom to the slaves. When it does come, do it. Dont [sic] hesitate."[17]

Twice in five months, Browning had suggested that under the law of war the slaves of rebels could legally be freed by military command. The same advice had been given him by other politicians, from the rough-hewn Erastus Wright[18] to the urbane Senator Sumner. No one, however, had laid out the reasoning behind these assertions in a way that might convince at least some of the legal experts and conservative politicians who were opposed to military emancipation.

Just over a week after Lincoln wrote his September 22 letter, Senator Sumner delivered a speech to the Massachusetts Republican Convention in which he cited his mentor, John Quincy Adams, as authority for the constitutional power to emancipate slaves in time of war. He repeated Adams's precedents from Latin America and the Seminole War, and added further examples from ancient history.[19] The senator had probably made the arguments to President Lincoln. However, reasons that were convincing to an abolitionist Republican from New England might not carry much weight with conservative Unionists from the border and Midwestern states.

Senator Orville Browning was just the kind of conservative supporter of the war who would have to be convinced that emancipation was a lawful military measure. In his own mind, Browning had apparently reconciled an emancipation proclamation with his conservative views of the Constitution. Lincoln needed to know how he had done this, because whatever arguments had persuaded Browning might well be effective with other conservative politicians. Lincoln also knew that the Illinois Republican Party had often relied on Browning to draft party platforms, convention resolutions, and other political documents.[20] Arguments advanced by Browning might well be expressed in artful language that the president could draw upon should he ever need to defend a future emancipation proclamation to the public.

For these reasons, Lincoln's September 22 letter went beyond its purported subject—emancipation by a military commander in the field—to raise the more fundamental constitutional question of the president's own powers. If the president was merely trying to convince Orville Browning that Frémont's action had been a legal and political error, there was no reason for him to suggest twice, as he did, that the legal limitations that applied to General Frémont applied equally to his own powers as commander in chief. This part of the letter implies that the issue of presidential power to emancipate slaves was already on Lincoln's mind in the fall of 1861, and that he wanted to know what Browning thought about it.

Perhaps the strongest reason to regard Lincoln's letter to Browning as primarily an effort to stimulate a reasoned reply is that this was how the recipient himself treated it. Browning was a vain man, who believed he was intellectually superior to Abraham Lincoln. Through his September 22 letter, the president had directly challenged him to demonstrate this supposed superiority. Browning's ego would not let him disregard the challenge. Browning's ambition may also have been a factor. In April, he had unsuccessfully sought an appointment to the Supreme Court. The president's letter of September 22 offered him a new opportunity to impress Lincoln with the range and depth of his legal knowledge, should another vacancy occur.

On September 30, Orville Browning sent Lincoln a fifteen-page reply, setting out in detail the reasoning behind his position. "With your permission," he wrote, "and with all deference to your opinions, so clearly expressed, I will venture, hastily to suggest my own views of the legal principles involved; for it is important that the law which governs the case should be certainly and clearly understood; and if you are right I am in very great error, which I ought to correct."[21]

Browning began by denying that Frémont's proclamation had violated the private property rights of American citizens or infringed the functions of Congress or the Missouri legislature. "It does not undertake to settle the rules of property between citizen and citizen. It does not deal with citizens at all, but with public enemies. It does not usurp a legislative function, but only declares a pre-existing law, and announces consequences which that law had already attached to given acts . . ."

According to Browning, neither Missouri property law nor Federal constitutional law applied to the situation General Frémont faced. Instead, his proclamation "had reference to a totally different class of cases, provided for long ago, by the political law of Nations." It was based on, and justified by, the international laws of war: "The Confederate States, and all who acknowledge allegiance to the Confederate States, . . . are public enemies. They are at war with the United States. Men taken in battle are held as prisoners; flags of truce pass between the hostile lines; intercourse is forbidden between certain States and parts of States; and sea-ports are formally blockaded. These things constitute war, and all the rules of war apply, and all belligerent rights attach." To define these belligerent rights, Browning quoted the following passages from the work of Jean Jacques Burlamaqui, an eighteenth-century professor of law at the University of Geneva:

> The state of war, into which the enemy has put himself, . . . permits of itself every method that can be used against him; so that he has no reason to complain whatever we do.
>
> As to the goods of the enemy, it is certain that the state of war permits us to carry them off, to ravage, to spoil, or even entirely to destroy them. . . .
>
> In general it certainly is not lawful to plunder for plunder's sake, but it is just and innocent only, when it bears some relation to the design of the war; that is when an advantage directly accrues from it to ourselves, by appropriating these goods, or at least, when by ravaging and destroying them, we in some measure weaken the enemy.[22]

"Is there any question," Browning went on to ask, "that the proclamation, carried into practical effect, would tend to our advantage by greatly weakening the enemy and diminishing his ability to carry on the war, and do us injury?"

By this point in his letter, Browning had gone far beyond his purported object of defending General Frémont's counterinsurgency decree. Frémont's order had been directed against property and slaves within Union lines, and thus under the military control of Frémont's own army. It was intended to punish individual Missouri slaveholders for guerrilla activities, not to weaken the Confederate war effort by depriving it of slave labor. Browning, too, seems to have realized that he and the president were now discussing matters far beyond the questionable political and legal judgment of John C. Frémont.

It is not usually noted that President Lincoln, in his September 22 letter, announced the legal justification he would eventually invoke to emancipate slaves in the Confederacy. When Lincoln wrote Senator Browning, the president did not argue that "military necessity" could never justify interference with slavery; rather, he claimed that he could not see any military necessity to justify the specific actions of General Frémont. Implicit in this criticism was the idea that an emancipation proclamation that did meet the test of military necessity would be both constitutionally and politically acceptable.

In the 1860s, the legal principle of military necessity was a new concept, only recently introduced into the law of war as a protection for private property owned by enemy civilians.[23] In 1812, Chief Justice John Marshall had declared that all personal property owned by the citizens of an enemy state could be seized and forfeited. By 1861, some authorities were beginning to suggest that private property should be respected in war unless there was a military necessity for its seizure or destruction. Henry Halleck, soon to be named the commanding general of all the Union armies, had adopted this approach to private property in his 1861 book on international law.[24] The commanding general in November 1861, George B. McClellan, would similarly advise a subordinate to respect the constitutional rights of hostile civilians, so far as "military necessity will permit."[25]

Lincoln would later appeal to this principle in the initial draft of an emancipation proclamation presented to his cabinet on July 22, 1862, when he referred to emancipation "as a fit and necessary military measure" to be used against the rebels. The final proclamation, signed on January 1, 1863, expressly declared the president's view that emancipation was "warranted by the Constitution, upon military necessity."

Jean Jacques Burlamaqui, as filtered through Orville Browning, presented President Lincoln with an expanded view of the scope of military necessity. In his September 22 letter the president had conceded that if a general needed to use private property for the benefit of his own forces, "for a pasture, an encampment, or a fortification," for example, then military necessity would legally justify the temporary seizure of that property. Browning's September 30 letter told him that the laws of war would authorize the seizure, and even the complete destruction, of private property, not only to benefit friendly forces, but also to weaken the resources of the enemy. Under this theory, the private property that could lawfully be destroyed included the "property" relationship between master and slave.

Browning's letter was filed in the White House for future use if the president ever decided to employ emancipation as a weapon against the rebels. Senator Sumner and others had already argued in general terms that the law of war allowed the president to emancipate the enemy's slaves. Now Senator Browning had provided a theoretical justification for such action by the commander in chief.

In his correspondence with General Frémont, President Lincoln implicitly approved the use of military commissions to punish unlawful combatants. Although the president ordered that no death sentences be carried out under the proclamation without his approval, he did not object in principle to the punishment of American citizens by military tribunals for violations of the laws of war.[26] Thereafter, military commission trials proceeded in Missouri with little interference from Washington.

In early 1862, further support for the use of military commissions came from George McClellan, then the Commanding General of the U.S. Army. On November 27, 1861, a U.S. Army patrol arrested seven citizens of Dranesville, Virginia, for killing two Union sentries and mutilating their bodies. Two more civilians were arrested on December 6 and sent to join the others in military custody at the Old Capitol prison in Washington, D.C. As with most other prisoners arrested on the East Coast in 1861, no further efforts were made to categorize them as prisoners of war, unlawful combatants, criminal suspects, or simply political prisoners.

The daughter of one of the men, John Farr, petitioned Secretary of State William Seward for her father's release, leading to an investigation of the incident by Allan Pinkerton, General McClellan's chief of intelligence. The results were not what Farr or his daughter had hoped for. On January 13, 1862, Pinkerton reported that Farr was a member of the Confederate Home Guard in Dranesville who had participated in the guerrilla party that murdered the two soldiers. He recommended that the "said John B. Farr be not released from custody, but that he be held until a military court can afford him trial for his manifold crimes."[27] Pinkerton's investigations continued until January 27, and on January

30, General McClellan ordered that all nine prisoners be "kept in close confinement until such time as they can be tried by a military commission for the crimes with which they stand charged."[28] Thereafter, however, General McClellan, preoccupied with preparing the Army of the Potomac for its spring campaign on the Virginia Peninsula, seems to have lost interest in the Dranesville affair. No trials were ever held before a military commission. Some of the nine prisoners were released later in the year; others were exchanged for pro-Union civilians held by the Confederacy.

Whatever doubts may have remained about whether the administration approved trials by military commissions were resolved by the new secretary of war, Edwin M. Stanton, on April 5, 1862. The secretary informed General Halleck in St. Louis that he had received notice of the results of two military commissions ordered by the general for communicating with the enemy and guerrilla activity, and that he "heartily approved" Halleck's actions. Further, the secretary wrote that "the form of procedure [used by Halleck] will be directed to be observed in all other departments in like cases."[29] The adjutant general of the army thereafter sent a copy of Halleck's action to General Frémont, then in command of the Mountain Department in western Virginia, noting that the secretary of war approved this form of procedure in like cases, "especially in regard to guerrillas."[30] It must have been especially galling to Frémont to have the actions of one of his successors in St. Louis praised by the secretary of war when his own decisions there had been so strongly criticized.

6

Congress Acts and the Confederacy Responds

By the spring of 1862, the Lincoln administration had, as a matter of policy, accorded Confederate forces all the rights of legitimate belligerents under the laws of war. Through military commissions, the administration was enforcing the laws of war against unlawful combatants for the Confederacy. The administration was not, however, asserting the full belligerent right to seize enemy property or free enemy slaves. To senators Orville Browning and Charles Sumner, it appeared obvious that the laws of war should apply to enemy property, including "slave property."

From where the president sat, the problem was more complex. For one thing, his was not the only voice speaking for the Federal government on this issue. Congress had enacted legislation on Confederate property, and both the scope and constitutional basis of this legislation was less than clear. As the president had pointed out to General John C. Frémont, for the military to declare the slaves of the rebels to be free would go beyond the terms of existing legislation, and might even violate those laws.

The restrictive policy on enemy slaves that President Lincoln required General Frémont to respect arose from precedents established by the War Department early in the Civil War in response to correspondence with General Benjamin Butler, a political general who owed his rank to his position as a prominent Massachusetts Democrat. In May 1861, Butler had been placed in command of Fortress Monroe, the Federally controlled enclave on the Chesapeake coast of Virginia.

Shortly after assuming command, Butler reported to army headquarters that he had just been faced with questions "of very considerable importance both in a military and political aspect," and requested the government's approval for the course he had taken. On May 23, three fugitives from slavery had approached the sentries at Fortress Monroe to seek refuge from their master, Colonel Charles Mallory. General Butler reported that he questioned them personally and "found satisfactory evidence that these men were about to be taken to Carolina for the purpose of aiding the secession forces there." One of the men also claimed he "had left his master from fear that he would be called upon to take part in the rebel armies." Furthermore, General Butler had been "credibly informed that the negroes in this neighborhood are now being employed in the erection of batteries and other works by the rebels, which it would be nearly or quite impossible to construct without their labor." Because he found the three fugitives to be "very serviceable," and he "had great need of labor in [the] quartermaster's department," Butler decided to use them in the service of the U.S. Army. Finally, he reported his intention to "send a receipt to Colonel Mallory that [he] had so taken them," as would be done "for any other property of a private citizen which the exigencies of the service seemed to require to be taken by [the army], and especially property that was designed, adapted, and about to be used against the United States."[1]

Had he, General Butler asked, acted properly under the circumstances? In other words, should the secessionists "be allowed the use of this property against the United States, and we not be allowed its use in aid of the United States?" Butler, with a lawyer's skill, had set out the strongest possible case for keeping these fugitives in U.S. custody. Retaining them would both hurt the enemy—by making it harder to fortify their positions near Fortress Monroe—and benefit the United States—by using the fugitives' labor in support of the fort's quartermaster.

Under nineteenth-century American law, these facts suggested at least two legal justifications for keeping the fugitives. First, property used in the commission of a crime could be seized and forfeited to the government. Slaves constructing Confederate fortifications might be considered property that was being used to help commit treason. Second, the Fifth Amendment to the Constitution allowed the Federal government to take private property for public purposes, if just compensation were paid. Working for the army quartermaster department would be a public purpose, and General Butler had reported that he was prepared to issue documentation to the slaves' owners to allow them to claim compensation for the labor "taken" from them.

Winfield Scott, the Commanding General of the Army, realized the political implications of Butler's questions. He forwarded the letter to the secretary of war for decision, noting that "there is much to praise in this report, and nothing to condemn. It is highly interesting in several aspects, particularly in its relation to the slave question."[2] Within five days, Butler received a reply from Secretary of War Simon Cameron himself:

SIR: Your action in respect to the negroes who came in your lines from the service of the rebels is approved.

The Department is sensible of the embarrassment which must surround officers conducting military operations in a State by the laws of which slavery is sanctioned. The Government cannot recognize the rejection by any State of its federal obligations nor can it refuse the performance of the federal obligations resting upon itself. Among these federal obligations, however, none can be more important than that of suppressing and dispersing armed combinations formed for the purpose of overthrowing its whole constitutional authority. While, therefore, you will permit no interference by the persons under your command with the relations of persons held to service under the laws of any State you will on the other hand so long as any State within which your military operations are conducted is under the control of such armed combinations refrain from surrendering to alleged masters any persons who may come within your lines. You will employ such persons in the service to which they may be best adapted, keeping an account of the labor by them performed, of the value of it and of the expense of their maintenance. The question of their final disposition will be reserved for future determination.[3]

The secretary of war's response was intended as a statement of general government policy, not simply local guidance for the commander of Fortress Monroe. The Butler–Cameron correspondence was released to the press and published in the widely circulated *Harper's Weekly*. (On the same page, *Harper's* reported that 450 fugitives had arrived at the fort by the middle of June, and that a slave uprising was expected soon.)[4]

The army again faced a refugee problem in the fall of 1861, after the capture of several islands and footholds on the coast of the Carolinas.

In dealing with "persons held to service under the laws of such States," the secretary of war ordered the local commanding officer to follow the guidance he had earlier given to General Butler. The commander was authorized to "in general avail yourself of the services of any persons, whether fugitives from labor or not, who may offer them to the National Government." He was directed to "assure all loyal masters that Congress will provide just compensation to them for the loss of the services of the persons so employed," as General Butler had proposed back in May. According to Secretary Cameron, these policies would "avoid all interference with the social systems or local institutions of every State, beyond that which insurrection makes unavoidable and which a restoration of peaceful relations to the Union under the Constitution will immediately remove."[5]

Nowhere in this directive, or in the earlier Butler–Cameron correspondence, did the terms "contrabands," "contraband of war," or any other phrase derived from the law of war, appear.[6] Nor was there any suggestion that the fugitives would become free as a result of fleeing to Fortress Monroe or other U.S. Army enclaves on the coast. The requirement that General Butler keep an account of the value of any labor they performed, and the expense of their maintenance, implies that the fugitives would remain bondsmen—property—under the laws of Virginia and the other slave states. If, as appeared possible in the middle of 1861, the secession crisis could still be settled by negotiation, presumably one of the minor issues to be resolved would be reimbursement of the slaves' owners for the value of the fugitives' work for the U.S. Army, minus the expense of keeping them. Secretary Cameron's statement that the "question of their final disposition will be reserved for future determination" certainly suggests that they might be returned to their masters as part of a peace settlement.

General Butler's policy was not a step toward emancipation. Rather, it was a reaffirmation that the Federal government was prepared to recognize and protect the rights of slaveholders, even if they lived in states that had rebelled against the authority of United States.

Butler's policy toward slavery was adopted, with refinements, by an act of Congress. Toward the end of the special session convened by President Lincoln on July 4, 1861, Congress adopted this policy against the Confederates in what became known as the First Confiscation Act.[7] Section 1 of the act said that "any property of whatsoever kind or description" used in support of the rebellion was to be the "lawful subject of prize and capture wherever found." Such property would be forfeited to the U.S. government after proceedings in Federal court to condemn the property.

The Constitution gave Congress the power to "declare War, . . . and make Rules concerning Captures on Land and Water"—that is, to define when and how the United States would exercise its war power over enemy property under the law of nations. The First Confiscation Act appeared to be an application of this constitutional power. The terms "prize" and "capture" had a customary meaning under the law of war— "prize" referring to the taking of enemy property at sea, and "capture" to similar proceedings on land. The use of these terms marked the first Congressional recognition that the property rights of rebels might no longer be protected by the Fifth Amendment and should be dealt with under the laws of war.

However, having implicitly asserted the right to treat the Confederates as enemies in war, subject to the law of war, Congress backed away from the full implications of this assertion. As Chief Justice John Marshall had declared in *Brown v. United States*, when the United States was at war, it had the right to take as its own any property of the enemy, including private property of enemy citizens. In August 1861, Congress was not yet willing to apply the full rigor of this rule to rebellious U.S. citizens.

The act therefore fell back on the old rule of English and American criminal law and authorized only the forfeiture of property actually used in support of the rebellion. Also, the property would be subject to forfeiture only if its owner "shall knowingly use or employ, or consent to the use or employment" of the property in support of the rebellion. Like a typical criminal statute, the act required both an evil result (helping the rebels) and a wrongful intent on the part of the person (the property owner) who contributed to that result. If the Taney Supreme Court eventually held that the Confederates could not be treated as enemies in war, the law would still be constitutional as an exercise of the congressional power to define and punish treason.

To remove any doubt that the act applied to slave property, Congressman Lyman Trumbull successfully offered an amendment in the form of a new section dealing specifically with slaves.[8] The new section 4 said that any master who "required or permitted" his or her slaves "to work or to be employed in or upon any fort, navy yard, dock, armory, ship, entrenchment, or in any military or naval service whatsoever" against the U.S. government, would thereby "forfeit his claim to such labor" in the future—that is, the master would lose his slave property.

The First Confiscation Act went beyond the policy developed by General Butler by providing a means to eliminate at least some rights of slaveholders in certain carefully defined cases. It did not, however, say what would become of enslaved persons thereafter. In particular, it did not grant them freedom. A slave whose master had forfeited his claim to the slave's labor might still remain a slave for other purposes. For example, the slave's children might still be owned by the former master, even if they were born after a Federal court had held that the master had forfeited any right to a slave's labor. The First Confiscation Act was designed more to punish slave owners than to free slaves.

If the former master no longer owned the right to a slave's labor, and if the slave had not been freed, who did own the right to that labor? In most situations, property forfeited by judgment of a Federal court due to the owner's misconduct became the property of the United States. If sections 1 and 4 of the Confiscation Act were widely enforced, would the U.S. government then find itself owning slaves? That would be an especially uncomfortable position for a Republican administration. President Lincoln assured Orville Browning, and perhaps others, that no one who had fled to Federal military lines would ever be returned to slavery.[9] However, under the U.S. Constitution, Congress, not the president, has the authority to dispose of government property. If the Democrats regained control of Congress, they could return forfeited slaves to their original owners as part of a compromise peace settlement.

Even without forfeiture proceedings, section 4 of the act could be used as a defense in a slave owner's suit to return fugitives to slavery under the Fugitive Slave Act of 1850. The last sentence of the Confiscation Act provided that in any suit to claim the return of a fugitive, "it shall be a full and sufficient answer to such claim that the person whose service or labor is claimed had been employed in hostile service against the Government of the United States, contrary to the provisions of this Act." Unfortunately, because suspected fugitives were not allowed to testify in their own defense at hearings under the Fugitive Slave Act, it would be very difficult for a fugitive to establish that he or she had been used in "hostile service" against the United States. Even if that fact could be established, the fugitive would then have to present evidence that his or her purported owner had voluntarily authorized this hostile service. Finally, even if section 4 of the Confiscation Act had, for all practical purposes, freed a fugitive whose labor had been used for hostile purposes, that section would not free the fugitive's children or spouse, or other refugees whose labor had not been used to support the enemy.

Considering its limitations, it is not surprising that very few slave owners forfeited their human property under the First Confiscation Act.[10] Attorney General Edward Bates has been faulted for failing to direct the appropriate U.S. attorneys to track down property (including refugees from slavery) that had been used to support the rebellion and take those cases to court. In fairness to Bates, it should be pointed out that Congress had given him authority over the U.S. attorneys only four days before the First Confiscation Act was passed.[11] Up until August 1861, the attorney general had had no administrative responsibilities, and the principal duty of his office had been to provide legal advice to the president and cabinet. The activities of the various U.S. attorneys had traditionally been coordinated by the secretary of state. This onerous responsibility had not been part of the job when Bates accepted the office of attorney general, and his lack of enthusiasm for carrying out his new duty is understandable.

Vigorous enforcement of the act was probably impractical anyway, at least as long as the war continued. Witnesses or other evidence were needed to establish that property at issue had been used in support of the Confederate war effort, and that the owner had authorized or permitted such use. Most of the cases would be heard in border slave states, where nonwhites were not allowed to testify as witnesses. Any white witnesses would probably be unavailable because they were behind the Confederate military lines (or in the Confederate army).

In an effort to enlist the aid of private citizens in enforcing the act, Congress borrowed an idea taken from British and American laws against smuggling. Section 3 provided that "any person may file an information" with the appropriate U.S. attorney, "in which case the proceedings shall be for the use of such informer and the United States in equal parts." In other words, the informer would get half the value of any forfeited property.

Even this offer failed to produce results. Citizens, including soldiers, who might be tempted to exploit section 3 of the act faced a risk of legal liability themselves if they interfered with the owner's rights but then failed to win in the forfeiture trial. As Colonel David Mitchell discovered after seizing Mr. Harmony's wagons during the Mexican War, you could be held liable for trespass to private property despite your honest belief that military reasons justified the seizure. At least one Union officer discovered after the Civil War that he could be held personally liable for having sheltered fugitive slaves before the Thirteenth Amendment abolished slavery.[12] General William Rosecrans warned military personnel under his command of the risks of seizing enemy property they believed was subject to forfeiture: "All property in transit between loyal and disloyal districts for trade, all that has been used to aid the rebels in arms, . . . or that is designed to be used in aid of men in rebellion is subject to prize and capture, but whoever undertakes to capture it does so at his peril, and he must bring it into the U.S. district court where the right of capture will be examined and decided."[13]

The army had its own good reasons for discouraging officers and soldiers from enforcing the Confiscation Act. Soldiers and officers allowed to attend a U.S. District Court hearing would be absent from their military duties. Because forfeited property became U.S. government property, the army would often end up with the responsibility of guarding and caring for it. Refugees from slavery, in particular, were almost always an unwelcome responsibility for field commanders, who had to provide food and shelter for them using supply lines that were already overburdened. For the army, enforcing the First Confiscation Act offered many burdens and few benefits.

The Confederate government quickly responded to the passage of the First Confiscation Act. For the Confederates, there was no question that the law of war applied to their relations with the United States, and Chief Justice Marshall (a Virginian, after all) had declared that a nation at war could take all property belonging to the enemy government or its citizens. It was therefore not surprising that on August 19, 1861, the Confederate Congress took up consideration of "An act for the forfeiture and confiscation of the estates, property and effects of alien enemies." Under section 1 of the act,

[all] the lands, tenements and hereditaments, goods and chattels, rights and credits within these Confederate States, and every right and interest therein held, owned, possessed or enjoyed by or for any alien enemy since the twenty-first day of May, eighteen hundred and sixty one, be, and the same are hereby, forfeited and confiscated by and for the Confederate

States of America, and especially for the full indemnity of any
true and loyal citizen or resident of these Confederate States . . .
for which he has suffered any loss or injury under the act of the
United States to which this act is retaliatory.[14]

The reference to "rights and credits" made it clear that this bill, if enacted, would wipe out all debts owed by Confederate citizens to Northern creditors. By seizing and forfeiting all property owned by U.S.
citizens in the South, the proposed law would have gone far beyond
the narrow terms of the Federal government's First Confiscation Act,
and would have invited further retaliation from the U.S. Congress.
It might also increase support for the war among key elements of
society in the Union, since only by winning the war could Northern
merchants, bankers, and other creditors collect debts owed by their
Confederate customers.

Cooler heads soon realized that the proposed act could have unfortunate consequences for the Confederacy. On August 22, the initial
bill was tabled and a more moderate draft substituted. Under this bill,
the property (including debts) of enemy aliens would not be forfeited.
Rather, it was to be "sequestered by the Confederate States of America"
and "held for the full indemnity" of any Confederate citizen or resident
who suffered loss under the First Confiscation Act, or any later legislation of the U.S. Congress. The sequestration bill passed and was signed
into law by Jefferson Davis on August 30, 1861.[15]

Compared with the Union's First Confiscation Act, the Confederate sequestration law was more comprehensive in scope and more restrained in impact. Whereas the Federal Confiscation Act was narrowly
targeted against property used for hostile purposes, the Confederate law
applied to all property of U.S. citizens. On the other hand, property
seized by the Confederate government would not be irrevocably lost
to its original owners. Instead, it would be held by the Confederate
government—"sequestered"—until needed to compensate Confederate
citizens, or until the end of hostilities. Any property of U.S. citizens still
sequestered at the end of a successful war for Confederate independence
could be used as a bargaining chip in peace negotiations. Sequestration,
rather than forfeiture, would also give U.S. citizens owning property in
the Confederacy a reason to pressure their government not to enforce
the First Confiscation Act, and might erode, rather than strengthen,
Northern support for the war. As a contribution to the development of

the international law of war, the Confederate approach to enemy alien property proved to be more advanced than the Union's confiscation acts. Sequestration, rather than forfeiture, of enemy alien property was later practiced by most of the belligerent powers in the world wars of the twentieth century.

7

Military Necessity and Lincoln's Concept of the War

The South's restrained response to the First Confiscation Act strengthened the political barriers to Lincoln's use of the emancipation weapon. Northerners holding property on Confederate territory could now be expected to join the white populations of the border states, Democrats, and conservative Republicans in opposing any Federal interference with "slave property" held by the enemy. In his letter to Orville Browning, President Lincoln had hinted that he might adopt an emancipation policy if he saw the military necessity for it. If the president and the Republicans were to remain in power, that necessity would have to be clear enough to overcome not only the political and legal qualms of conservative politicians, but also the financial interests of businessmen and investors with sequestered property subject to Confederate forfeiture proceedings.

The military necessity for emancipation would also have to be strong enough to have at least a chance of withstanding judicial scrutiny. As a lawyer, the president knew that any emancipation policy he ordered the army to adopt would eventually be reviewed in court and that, if the courts held the policy to be illegal, the Federal officers who enforced it could be held personally liable to reimburse aggrieved slaveholders for the loss of their property. Roger Taney, author of the *Dred Scott* decision, was still chief justice of the United States, and a majority of his Supreme Court were Southerners who would not be inclined to look with favor on a presidential attempt to interfere with slavery. They might, however, grudgingly respect a presidential finding of military necessity under the law of war. In the case of *Luther v. Borden*, Taney had accepted that the law of war applied to the Rhode Island governor's suppression of a rebellion within that state, while warning that "no more force . . . can be used than is *necessary* to accomplish" that objective.[1]

The correspondence between the president and Senator Browning had identified two possible foundations for a finding of military necessity—weakening the Confederate war effort or strengthening that of the Union. These ideas were consistent with President Lincoln's own view of the war as primarily a problem of physics and geometry, requiring the application of superior force at the correct places in order for the North to prevail.

Lincoln's mind was naturally drawn to this kind of quantitative and geometrical analysis. A surveyor before he turned to the law, in later life he studied Euclid's *Geometry* for pleasure. When most Americans reflected on Niagara Falls, they thought of the beauty of the scene and of the awe it inspired. Lincoln, unromantically, focused on calculating the physical power that the mass of water passing over the Falls represented, and how those calculations could be used to estimate the age of the Falls and to comprehend the power of the sun to evaporate and lift into the sky the tons of water that poured over them.[2]

President Lincoln first expressed his "general idea of the war" as an engineering problem to be solved by the marshaling and correct application of superior physical power in January 1862, in a letter to one of his generals in the West: "I state my general idea of this war to be that we have the *greater* numbers, and the enemy has the *greater* facility of concentrating forces upon points of collision; that we must fail, unless we can find some way of making *our* advantage an overmatch for *his;* and this can only be done by menacing him with superior forces at *different* points, at the same time. . . ."[3] He stated the concept more succinctly two years later, in reply to a critic of the Emancipation Proclamation and the government's use of colored troops: "It is not a question of sentiment or taste, but one of physical force, which may be measured, and estimated as horse-power and steam-power are measured and estimated."[4]

In a book published in 1890, one of the president's secretaries, William O. Stoddard, claimed that after the Union defeat at Fredericksburg Lincoln had told him, "if the same battle were to be fought over again, every day, through a week of days, with the same relative results, the army under Lee would be wiped out to its last man, the Army of the Potomac would still be a mighty host [and] the war would be won. . . ."[5] There are reasons to doubt the accuracy of this quotation. It was published almost thirty years after it was supposedly made, the wording does not sound like Lincoln, and the idea expressed seems more appropriate to the bloody Overland Campaign two years later than to the 1862 battle of Fredericksburg. (In 1862, the army suffered greater losses at Shiloh and Antietam than it did at Fredericksburg.) Nevertheless, the general concept Stoddard attributed to the president—that superior physical power would eventually prevail despite, or even as a result of, a series of tactical defeats—seems in accord with Lincoln's mature military thinking. Stoddard may well have heard something like this in the Lincoln White House.

In war, a policy might benefit one side or hurt the other, but still not be strictly necessary to influence the outcome of the conflict. How could a Federal government policy of emancipation meet the requirement of being a "military necessity" for restoring the Union? And how could a wartime president convince the American people that such a necessity existed?

In the mid-nineteenth century, an American lawyer seeking answers to these questions would turn to the debate about a similar phrase in the U.S. Constitution. Article 1 of the Constitution grants a list of specific legislative powers to Congress—to coin money, and to raise armies, for example. It then goes on to give Congress the additional power to make any law "necessary and proper" to carrying out the specific grants of power. From the earliest days of the Republic, there were two approaches to the interpretation of the "necessary and proper" clause, and these could easily be applied by analogy to the "military necessity" principle.

Chief Justice John Marshall supported a broad interpretation of the necessary and proper clause that would widen as far as possible the scope of legitimate congressional action. "Let the end be legitimate," Marshall wrote in 1819, "and all means which are appropriate, which are plainly adapted to that end, which are not prohibited but consist with the letter and spirit of the constitution, are constitutional."[6] In politics, this broad interpretation was adopted by the Federalist, Whig, and Republican parties to provide constitutional underpinning for the Federal funding of "internal improvements" (building roads, canals, and railroads) and the creation of national banking institutions. As a long-time Whig, Abraham Lincoln would naturally be inclined to follow this broad interpretation.

Thomas Jefferson held a narrower view of the necessary and proper clause. For Jefferson, the exercise of legislative power was not "necessary" merely because it was "convenient." The only measures that were truly necessary were those "without which the grant of power [to Congress] would be nugatory."[7] Jefferson's view of constitutional necessity was later associated with President Andrew Jackson and the Democratic Party, and Jackson relied on this theory when he vetoed legislation to recharter the Bank of the United States. Creating a bank, he told Congress, was not necessary to the exercise of any specific power granted to the Federal government. The Jefferson/Jackson interpretation was later used by the Democrats to oppose tariffs protecting infant American industries and the Federal funding of internal improvements.

Lincoln served his political apprenticeship in Illinois by opposing the policies of Andrew Jackson, and the Republican Party had inherited the internal improvement and high-tariff policies of the Whig party. When forced to think about military necessity and its role in American law, the members and supporters of the Lincoln administration would, by analogy to their sympathies in the debate on the necessary and proper clause, naturally lean toward a broad or even loose interpretation of what military necessity permitted. Republican senator Orville Browning had already told the president that, in his opinion, the law of war allowed the commander in chief to do almost anything that would hurt the enemy or help the government.

For most purposes, Lincoln's conduct of the Civil War reflected this expansive interpretation of military necessity. At a cabinet meeting on July 22, 1862, for example, the president approved orders allowing army commanders, when operating in rebel territory, to take any private property "which may be necessary or convenient for their commands, for supplies or other military purposes," and to have private property "destroyed, for proper military purposes." Although no Federal official would believe he had the right to take such measures in peacetime, they were all well within the broad principle of necessity embraced by Senator Browning in September.

When the issue was emancipation, however, Lincoln applied a stricter, "Jeffersonian" standard of necessity. That is, an emancipation proclamation would only be issued when it appeared to the president that without it, the Union's war effort would be rendered "nugatory." On July 13, 1862, the president told navy secretary Gideon Welles and Secretary of State William Seward that "he had about come to the conclusion that we must free the slaves or be ourselves subdued." In 1872, Welles recalled that during this conversation Lincoln had called emancipation "a military necessity, absolutely essential to the preservation of the Union."[8] The president continued to defend the proclamation as an absolute necessity after it had been issued. Francis B. Carpenter wrote that in 1864 the president told him that he issued the Emancipation Proclamation because he "felt that we had reached the end of our rope. . . ; that we had about played our last card and must change our tactics or lose the game." Later, Lincoln told the British orator George Thomson that he had acted "in the last extremity" because he "felt that slavery must die that the nation might live."[9]

Abolitionists found it frustrating that Lincoln adopted a stricter standard of military necessity for emancipation than for other measures against enemy property. From the president's viewpoint, however, it was reasonable to require that emancipation be based on the clearest and most pressing evidence of military necessity. With a Federal court system still dominated by Southern judges, emancipation was the war measure most likely to be struck down as unconstitutional. Of greatest importance, once the North adopted a policy of military emancipation, the president knew that any chance for a negotiated peace based on "the Union as it was" would end. The killing would go on, relentlessly, until one side or the other was utterly defeated.

In the spring of 1862, the Union military situation was hardly "in the last extremity." George McClellan, the new General in Chief of the Army, had created a formidable fighting machine in the Army of the Potomac, and was preparing to move that army up the Virginia Peninsula to attack the Confederate capital at Richmond. In the West, Brigadier General Ulysses Grant had gained control of the Tennessee and Cumberland rivers through his capture of Fort Henry and Fort Donelson, forcing the Confederates to evacuate Kentucky and most of Tennessee. By April 3, Secretary of War Edwin Stanton had become so optimistic that he halted all Federal recruiting, closed all the recruiting offices, and ordered the office furniture sold.

Stanton's optimism received a check on April 6, when the Confederates attacked Grant's army at Shiloh, Tennessee, inflicting 13,000 Federal casualties.[10] The Union's fortunes appeared to have recovered by the end of June, however, when the Army of the Potomac reached the outskirts of Richmond. In the West, U.S. forces had advanced into northern Mississippi at Corinth and captured the strategic Island No. 10 in the Mississippi River. On June 28, President Lincoln wrote that, in his "view of the present condition of the War," raising only 100,000 more soldiers to help McClellan take Richmond would "substantially end the war."[11] With the Union about to win the war, there was no foreseeable military necessity that could legally justify an emancipation proclamation.

In the fall of 1861, military necessity required the president to actively oppose emancipation as a means of keeping Kentucky in the Union. The fall of Fort Henry and Fort Donelson in 1862 removed this necessity by bringing Kentucky firmly within the military control of the U.S. Army. During the dispute with Frémont about emancipation in Missouri, Lincoln must have found it galling to be forced, by military necessity, to intervene to protect slavery. From now on he could take a more relaxed approach when military commanders tinkered with the institution in other theaters of war.

Slavery and Martial Law: The Hunter Doctrine

On March 31, 1862, General David Hunter took command of the U.S. Army Department of the South, which consisted mainly of islands and a few enclaves along the Atlantic coast of Georgia and the Carolinas. Like John Frémont, Hunter was one of the few abolitionists to have served as an officer in the peacetime Regular Army. Both men were impulsive and, from a strictly military standpoint, neither was a very good general. Profiting from Frémont's experience, however, Hunter had thought more deeply about the laws governing military emancipation.

Even before he took command of his new department, Hunter began complaining that the department had too few troops assigned to it, at one point claiming that his 16,000 men faced 65,000 Confederates.[12] Although the Department of the South had too few soldiers, it also had a large African American population of unclear status, both refugees from slavery and slaves whose white masters had fled upon the approach of Union forces. General Hunter decided to draw on this population to remedy his lack of troops and to engage in some experiments to see how far the administration would allow him to go toward emancipation of the slaves in his department. Later in 1862, his commander in chief would benefit from some of these experiments.

Hunter began the experiments after the Confederates surrendered Fort Pulaski, at the mouth of the Savannah River, to forces under his command. On April 13, 1862, General Hunter issued an official decla-

ration that "all persons of color lately held to involuntary service by enemies of the United States in Fort Pulaski and on Cockspur Island, Ga.,
are hereby confiscated and declared free in conformity with law, and
shall hereafter receive the fruits of their own labor."[13] Hunter claimed
to have acted "in conformity with law," though he carefully avoided
specifying the laws involved. The law of war was certainly part of the
foundation for his action, but if challenged he, unlike Frémont, could
also rely on a specific act of Congress for authority.

As a paymaster in the prewar army, Hunter was familiar with the
statutes governing the handling of government property. The Constitution gave Congress power to make laws governing captured property
and rules for the land and naval forces. In 1806, Congress exercised
both powers when it revised the Articles of War governing discipline in
the army. As part of the revision, they passed Article of War 58, which
said that "all public stores taken in the enemy's camp, towns, forts, or
magazines, whether of artillery, ammunition, clothing, forage or provisions, shall be secured for the service of the United States. . . ."[14]

Under the laws of Georgia, of course, slaves were property. General
Hunter could reasonably claim that as the general in command of forces
that had just captured Fort Pulaski, he was entitled to assume that all
enslaved persons found on the territory surrendered by the enemy were
Confederate "public stores." By freeing these slaves, he had "secured"
them for the service of the United States. Giving them freedom ensured
that they would not be tempted to return to their homes in Confederate
territory, and the April 13 order secured them for the service of the U.S.
Army by providing that any of these "persons of color as are able bodied
and may be required shall be employed in the quartermaster's department
at the rates heretofore established" by Hunter's predecessor in command.

Hunter waited for a reaction from the Northern public and the government in Washington. There was none.[15] He prepared to take the
next step. In October 1861, the War Department had given Hunter's
predecessor instructions on the handling of refugees from slavery. "You
will employ such persons," Secretary Simon Cameron had written, "in
such services as they may be fitted for—either as ordinary employees,
or, if special circumstances seem to require it, in any other capacity, with
such organization (in squads, companies, or otherwise) as you may deem
most beneficial to the service; this, however, not being a general arming
of them for military service."[16]

Under this guidance, Hunter could reasonably claim that he was authorized to impose a military organization on the refugees he employed. The prohibition on "general arming" of these organizations could be read as authorizing the arming of *some* members of these quasi-military units. Hunter took these ambiguous instructions and ran with them. He had repeatedly told Washington that he needed more soldiers. When his superiors did not respond, Hunter took matters into his own hands by organizing and arming African American military units in the Department of the South.

Hunter took the final step on May 9, 1862, when he issued an emancipation proclamation for the area under his command. Far from being cowed by Frémont's fate, Hunter went beyond his proclamation to declare all slaves in the Department of the South to be "forever free," not just those belonging to disloyal masters:

> The three States of Georgia, Florida and South Carolina, comprising the Military Department of the South, having deliberately declared themselves no longer under the protection of the United States of America and having taken up arms against the said United States it becomes a military necessity to declare them under martial law. This was accordingly done on the 25th day of April, 1862. Slavery and martial law in a free country are altogether incompatible; the persons in these three States—Georgia, Florida and South Carolina—heretofore held as slaves are therefore declared forever free.[17]

Here Hunter made a rather subtle legal argument, one that he probably thought distinguished his action from Frémont's. In the Civil War era, "martial law" was often used as another name for the law of war, especially with respect to the law of war governing military rule of territory occupied by a hostile army. The law of war, in turn, was believed to be based on the "laws of nature"—those rules, based on human reason, that ought to be observed even by independent nations or peoples with no sovereign governing them. In 1863, for example, the U.S. Army's official codification of the law of war declared that "there exists no law or body of authoritative rules of action between hostile armies, except that branch of the law of nature and nations which is called the law and usages of war on land." In the decade after the Civil War, the U.S. Supreme Court often reaffirmed that the law of war was based on reason and the law of nature.[18]

Slavery was thought to be a legal institution that existed only under the local laws of individual nations or states. It was not authorized by the law of nations. In an 1825 decision of the Supreme Court, Chief Justice John Marshall, a Virginian and a slaveholder, had conceded that it could "scarcely be denied" that slavery was "contrary to the law of nature," under which "every man has a natural right to the fruits of his own labor."[19] More recently, Lincoln had rhetorically asked, "is not slavery universally granted to be, in the abstract, a gross outrage on the law of nature?"[20]

If martial law (derived from the law of nature) applied throughout the Department of the South, and if slavery was inconsistent with the law of nature, then, General Hunter reasoned, every slave in that department must be regarded as free (at least in the eyes of the Federal government) as soon as martial law applied. Under this logic, Hunter could argue that he was actually claiming an authority much more modest than Frémont had. His General Order of May 9, 1862, was not an attempt to punish rebels, free slaves, forfeit property, or otherwise act on matters within the authority of Congress or the state legislatures, as General Frémont had tried to do. Hunter was only recognizing something that had already occurred—the enemy's slaves had automatically been freed as soon as martial law applied throughout the department.

General Hunter's reasoning was legally unsophisticated as well as politically naïve. The foremost American authority on the law of war, Dr. Francis Lieber of Columbia College, criticized Hunter's proclamation on technical grounds. "Martial law," as General Hunter had used the term, applied only in territories actually under the control of the U.S. Army. Therefore, Dr. Lieber concluded, Hunter could not legitimately invoke martial law to free slaves in his entire department, most of which was still in Confederate hands.[21]

The political reaction came on May 19, 1862, when President Lincoln issued his own proclamation disapproving of Hunter's action. The president's public position on military emancipation had advanced considerably since September 1861. General Hunter's emancipation proclamation was not reversed as an act of "dictatorship," beyond the scope of military law. Instead, the president acted because "neither General Hunter, nor any other commander, or person, has been authorized by the Government of the United States, to make proclamations declaring the slaves of any State free." As a result, the proclamation was declared to be "altogether void" in the eyes of the U.S. government.

Instead of rejecting outright the legality of military emancipation, the president announced that "whether it be competent for me, as Commander-in-Chief of the Army and Navy, to declare the Slaves of any state or states, free, and whether at any time, in any case, it shall have become a necessity indispensable to the maintenance of the government, to exercise such supposed power, are questions which, under my responsibility, I reserve to myself."[22] For the first time, Lincoln had publicly suggested the legal standard he believed would justify military emancipation—"a necessity indispensable to the maintenance of the government."

Curiously, the president's proclamation was never officially transmitted to General Hunter through War Department channels.[23] Hunter knew that department commanders received their orders through official channels, not from the newspapers. Here the message between the lines was that the administration did not really care much about what Hunter did in an obscure theater of war, but it cared a great deal about what the public thought he was doing. The proclamation was an exercise in public relations, not a military order to change activities on the ground in the Department of the South. By July, the president was telling state governors that he still valued Hunter "for agreeing with me in the general wish that all men everywhere, could be free," and that he had only repudiated Hunter's emancipation decree because the general "expected more good, and less harm, from the measure, than I could believe would follow."[24] There was good reason for General Hunter to be on Lincoln's mind at that time. In July, the president was starting to draft an emancipation proclamation of his own, one that would incorporate some of the most radical features of Hunter's order.

McClellan Fails and Military Necessity Appears

The military situation had shifted alarmingly by the first half of July 1862. On June 25, Robert E. Lee launched a series of attacks on the Army of the Potomac that would, over a period of seven days, force it back from Richmond to Harrison's Landing on the James River, where it lay idle for weeks.

A military necessity for emancipation was becoming more credible. Even before the full scope of General George McClellan's defeat had become apparent, Lincoln was preparing to call on the state governors to raise 100,000 more troops. At the beginning of July, after the end of the Seven Days' Battles, it was clear that the Confederacy was still too strong, and the U.S. Army not quite strong enough, to bring the war to a close.

From July 7 to 9, the president visited the beaten Army of the Potomac on the Virginia Peninsula to assess for himself the prospects for future success in that theater. While he was there, General McClellan handed him a letter in which the general explained to Lincoln his views of the military situation and the future course of the war. McClellan, who had earlier charged that the Lincoln administration had not done enough to support his army, may have thought the letter to have been conciliatory, and hoped it would bring about his reinstatement as general in chief of the U.S. Army. He expressed support for a vigorous application of the president's war power against the rebellion. "This rebellion has assumed the character of a War," he determined, and "The Constitution gives you power sufficient even for the present terrible exigency." He also agreed with the president that destruction of the Confederate army, not the capture of Richmond, should be the main objective: "The policy of the Government must be supported by concentrations of military power. The national forces should not be dispersed . . . but should be mainly collected into masses and brought to bear upon the Armies of the Confederate States; those Armies thoroughly defeated, the political structure which they support would soon cease to exist."

The general expressed his support for military enforcement of the First Confiscation Act: "Slaves contraband under the Act of Congress, seeking military protection, should receive it." Although he opposed "forcible abolition of slavery," McClellan then conceded that military necessity could justify involuntary but *compensated* emancipation by the Federal government: "The right of the Government to appropriate permanently to its own service claims to slave labor should be asserted and the right of the owner to compensation therefore should be recognized. This principle might be extended upon grounds of military necessity and security to all the slaves within a particular state—and in Missouri, perhaps in Western Virginia also and possibly even in Maryland the expediency of such a military measure is only a question of time."[25]

Abraham Lincoln had recently been arguing for Federal funding of compensated emancipation in the loyal slave states, and General McClellan had no reason to believe these views would be unpalatable to the president. In fact they were little different from the limited view of military necessity Lincoln had expressed to Orville Browning the previous September. That was perhaps the real problem with McClellan's letter—for the president, there was nothing new in it.

Back in January, Lincoln had concluded that "we must fail, unless we can find some way of making *our* advantage an overmatch for *his*; and this can only be done by menacing [the enemy] with superior forces at *different* points, at the same time. . . ."[26] Something further had to be done to strengthen the Union forces or weaken those of the Confederacy, and McClellan had no new ideas on how to do this. The president had already decided to increase his call for new troops to 300,000, but this might not be enough to "overmatch" the Confederacy's geographical advantages. An emancipation proclamation might both diminish the support that slave labor gave to the Confederate war effort and encourage individual slaves to labor in support of the Union, but McClellan was incapable of making this calculation, or of finding any alternative way to increase military pressure on the enemy. The military justification for an emancipation proclamation was becoming increasingly apparent.

During a carriage ride to a funeral on July 13, only a few days after returning to Washington, Lincoln first revealed to Gideon Welles and William Seward that he "had given it much thought and . . . had about come to the conclusion that we must free the slaves or ourselves be subdued."[27] A week later, on July 21, he called a surprise cabinet meeting. (The summons struck Treasury Secretary Salmon Chase as a "novelty," since it had been so long since the previous meeting.) The president told the meeting he was "profoundly concerned at the present aspect of affairs, and had determined to take some definitive steps in respect to military action and slavery."[28] As a preliminary issue, the cabinet discussed the president's proposals to allow the army to live off the land when in rebel territory, seizing food and fodder and using the labor of fugitive slaves. The next morning, the cabinet met again and unanimously approved these measures, whereupon the president announced his intention to issue an emancipation proclamation, and presented his draft to the cabinet.

This initial draft played down military necessity as a legal basis for emancipation, mentioning it only in the last sentence. Instead, Lincoln sought to give the impression that he was acting on the authority of an act of Congress, the Second Confiscation Act, which had been passed after his conversation with Welles and Seward:

In pursuance of the sixth section of the act of congress entitled "An act to suppress insurrection and to punish treason and rebellion, to seize and confiscate property of rebels, and for other purposes" Approved July 17. 1862, and which act, and the Joint Resolution explanatory thereof, are herewith published, I, Abraham Lincoln, President of the United States, do hereby proclaim to, and warn all persons within the contemplation of said sixth section to cease participating in, aiding, countenancing, or abetting the existing rebellion, or any rebellion against the government of the United States, and to return to their proper allegiance to the United States, on pain of the forfeitures and seizures, as within and by said sixth section provided—

Section 6 of the Second Confiscation Act, to which the president referred, stated that "if any person . . . being engaged in armed rebellion against the government of the United States . . . shall not, within sixty days after public warning and proclamation duly given and made by the President of the United States . . . return to his allegiance to the United States, all the estate and property of such person shall be liable to seizure" by the U.S. government through lawsuits in the Federal courts.[29] The First Confiscation Act had authorized the government to confiscate property actually used (or intended to be used) to aid or promote rebellion. The Second Confiscation Act directed attention away from whether specific pieces of property had been used to support the rebellion and focused on the insurrectionary activities of property owners. Persons supporting the Confederacy would now face the seizure of *all* their property, wherever located and whatever it had been used for.

The constitutional basis for section 6 was unclear. The Constitution gave Congress the power to define the punishments for treason, but as a punishment for treason there were serious constitutional problems with section 6, many of which were brought to Lincoln's attention before he signed the Second Confiscation Act. One problem was that section 6 applied to people who were already "engaged in armed rebellion against the government" at the time the act was passed. The act could therefore be read as a "bill of attainder"—that is, an unconstitutional attempt by Congress to usurp the judicial function of punishing as crimes acts that had already been committed. Senator Orville Browning, for one, believed that section 6 was unconstitutional on that ground.[30] Thomas Ewing, a prominent Ohio lawyer and politician, wrote Lincoln that in "the opinion of nine tenths of the Bar" the act was "clearly uncon-stitutional" because it allowed forfeiture of all the property belonging to someone who had never been convicted of a crime.[31] The president himself threatened to veto the act because he believed it might violate the Constitution's provision that treason could not be punished by for-feiture of land and other real property for longer than the life of the individual traitor. (He signed the act after Congress passed a resolution clarifying that it had not intended that result.) The constitutionality of section 6 was not finally settled until a decade after the Civil War ended, when the Supreme Court held that it was not a punishment for treason but rather a legitimate exercise of the Federal government's power to seize enemy property under the law of war.[32]

Having threatened the rebels with loss of property, as required by a possibly unconstitutional section of the Confiscation Act, Lincoln next mentioned his intention to continue seeking Federal financing for state programs of compensated emancipation. As a former Whig, Lin-coln had long backed government spending for internal improvements. What better improvement could the Federal government finance than the elimination of slavery by the states that still had it? Lincoln had convinced himself that if the loyal border states (Delaware, Missouri, Maryland, and Kentucky) voluntarily moved to abolish slavery, this would undermine the morale of secessionists further South. So far, he had not been able to convince anyone else of this, and the responses from the border states had ranged from hostility to apathy. The presi-dent decided, however, to try once again: "And I hereby make known that it is my purpose, upon the next meeting of Congress, to again rec-ommend the adoption of a practical measure for tendering pecuniary aid to the free choice or rejection, of any and all States which may then be recognizing and practically sustaining the authority of the United States, and which may then have voluntarily adopted, or thereafter may voluntarily adopt, gradual abolishment of slavery within such State or States."

In the final phrase of his draft the president announced his inten-tion to adopt a sweeping emancipation policy. The object of the war, he reassured readers, was "to practically restore . . . the constitutional relation between the general government, and each, and all the states, wherein that relation is now suspended, or disturbed": "And, as a fit and necessary military measure for effecting this object, I, as Commander-in-Chief of the Army and Navy of the United States, do order and declare that on the first day of January in the year of our Lord one thousand, eight hundred and sixty three, all persons held as slaves within any state or states, wherein the constitutional authority of the United States shall not then be practically recognized, submitted to, and maintained, shall then, thenceforward, and forever, be free." Although the president claimed to be acting under his powers "as Commander-in-Chief of the Army and Navy of the United States," and declared his belief that emancipation was now a military necessity, he was not yet willing to publicly claim that the commander in chief's power to emancipate derived from the government's right to apply the law of war to the rebels. At this point in the war, his reticence is understandable.

Senators Sumner and Browning, among others, advised him that the law of war permitted him to free enemy slaves, but the Supreme Court had not yet ruled that the United States could resort to all means permitted by the law of war to defeat the Confederates. Chief Justice Taney's Court might still hold that the law of war did not apply during the Civil War. If so, and if the emancipation proclamation expressly said it was based on the law of war, then the Federal courts might decide that the proclamation was utterly void, and that those purportedly freed by the proclamation were still property.

If, on the other hand, the proclamation did not say by what constitutional authority the president (and Congress) acted, then the courts *might* regard the emancipations as a valid taking of property by the government under some other legal doctrine. They might, for example, hold that at least some slaves had been freed by the president's act, but then also decide that government must compensate their former owners for "taking" their property as required by the Fifth Amendment to the Constitution.

A presidential declaration of military necessity might also protect individual officers who enforced the proclamation against lawsuits by affected slave owners. Even Chief Justice Taney had conceded, in his opinion in *Mitchell v. Harmony,* that where "the necessity [was] urgent for the public service, such as will not admit of delay," the U.S. government would still be "bound to make full compensation to the owner" for property taken by the military, but the individual army officer who took the property could not be sued.[33] All in all, it was best for the president to declare there was a military necessity for emancipation, but not to mention the law of war.

The final words of Lincoln's July draft—"forever be free"—referred the reader back to the Second Confiscation Act. Section 9 of the act provided that "all slaves of persons who shall hereafter be engaged in rebellion . . . escaping . . . and taking refuge within the lines of the army . . . shall be deemed captives of war, and shall be *forever free* of their servitude, and not again held as slaves." (Emphasis added.)

The president had good rhetorical and legal reasons to quote the Confiscation Act at both the beginning and the end of his proclamation. As drafted, the proclamation left the reader with the impression that the president was merely carrying out a recently passed act of Congress, thereby fulfilling his constitutional duty to see that the laws were faithfully executed. Politically, this would make his proclamation sound less radical than it was.

The proclamation stood a better chance of surviving attack in the Federal courts if it appeared to be based not only on the president's war powers as commander in chief, but also on the will of Congress. During the War of 1812, the Supreme Court had ruled that the Federal government had the right, under the law of war, to seize enemy-owned property located within the territory of the United States at the beginning of a war, but it had also held that this power could only be exercised in accordance with an act of Congress, not just a decision of the executive branch of government. Lincoln had often stated that the Southern states had no legal right to secede, so that the entire area under Confederate control was, in the view of his administration, still legally the territory of the United States. Being able to link an emancipation proclamation to the war powers of both Congress and the president might make the proclamation easier to defend in court.

In fact, the president's draft announced a policy that went far beyond the strict terms of the Second Confiscation Act. Section 9 of the act had made the slaves of rebels free as soon as they came within the control of the Union army. The president, on the other hand, declared that at the beginning of 1863 he would free all slaves in areas still controlled by the Confederates, whether or not their owners supported the rebellion.

The president could nevertheless claim that his Emancipation Proclamation would carry out the underlying purposes of the Second Confiscation Act, even as it went beyond the words in section 9 of the act. By passing the act, it could be argued that Congress was adopting a policy of weakening the Confederate war economy by encouraging, through the promise of freedom, the desertion of the slaves whose labor supported that economy. In accordance with the policies proposed by Lincoln on July 21 and adopted by his cabinet on July 22, these refugees could then be employed as free laborers in support of the Union war effort. Congress had adopted emancipation as a means of economic warfare, and the president would carry this policy to its logical conclusion.

The administration was adopting policies on slavery that conformed to Burlamaqui's concept of military necessity and John Quincy Adams's constitutional theories. Under the former, the law of war allowed a government to do anything that would help its side or hurt the enemy. The Constitution, according to Adams, gave the Federal government the power to deal with slavery in any manner that would help strengthen its war effort or harm those of an enemy.

On July 28, the president explained to an official in occupied Louisiana how changes in policy toward fugitive slaves, even those belonging to "loyal" owners, could strengthen the Union military effort:

> Mr. Durant complains that in various ways the relation of master and slave is disturbed by the presence of our Army; and he considers it particularly vexatious that this, in part, is done under cover of an act of Congress, while constitutional guarantees are suspended on the plea of military necessity. The truth is, that what is done, and omitted, about slaves, is done and omitted on the same military necessity. It is a military necessity to have men and money; and we can get neither, in sufficient numbers, or amounts, if we keep from, or drive from our lines slaves coming to them.[34]

Soon thereafter, General Henry Halleck, the Commanding General of the U.S. Army, explained to a subordinate how a policy encouraging slaves to defect could weaken the Confederate war economy:

> The population of African descent that cultivate the lands and perform the labor of the rebels constitute a large share of their military strength, and enable the white masters to fill the rebel armies and wage a cruel and murderous war against the people of the Northern States. By reducing the laboring strength of the rebels their military power will be reduced. You are therefore authorized by every means in your power to withdraw from

the enemy their laboring force and population, and to spare no effort consistent with civilized warfare to weaken, harass, and annoy them, and to establish the authority of the Government of the United States within your department.[35]

The Lincoln administration had been working out a military rationale for emancipation for months before the preliminary proclamation was issued.

As a matter of strict logic, of course, an offensive emancipation policy based on the need to build up resources available to the Union and deplete those available to its enemies could only apply to slaves still under Confederate control. As even General McClellan recognized, in areas under Federal control the army could hire or requisition the labor of local slaves without offering them freedom. The promise of freedom could, however, be used to induce slaves under Confederate control to flee to areas under Union control. This placed a significant limit on the president's legal power to use emancipation as a weapon. Lincoln later had to explain this distinction to Treasury Secretary Chase after the final Emancipation Proclamation had been issued. "The original Proclamation has no constitutional or legal justification except as a military measure," the president wrote. "The exemptions were made because the military necessity did not apply to the exempted localities . . . If I take the step [you suggest] must I not do so, without the argument of military necessity, and so, without any argument, except the one that I think the measure politically expedient and morally right? Would I thus not give up all footing upon constitution or law? . . . Could it fail to be perceived that without any further stretch, I might . . . change any law in any state?"[36] These questions may not have been merely rhetorical. As he had done with Orville Browning, Lincoln may have been trying to goad the future chief justice into providing constitutional arguments that would have allowed him to free slaves in areas under Union control. If so, Salmon Chase failed the test.

By itself, section 9 of the Second Confiscation Act was a very imperfect means to weaken the South through emancipation. It made no promise of freedom to fugitives whose masters were not supporters of the rebellion, or to those who were technically owned not by disloyal men but rather by their wives or children. A spouse's or child's property rights were not, and under the Constitution could not be, affected by an act of treason by a husband or father. Lincoln, as a lawyer, was fully aware of this distinction, which he later made clear in a letter to the commanding general of the Department of Arkansas:

> It would appear . . . that Mrs. Mary E. Morton is the owner, independently of her husband, of a certain building, premises and furniture, which she, with her children, has been occupying and using peaceably during the war, until recently, when the Provost-Marshal has, in the name of the U.S. Government, seized the whole of said property, and ejected her from it. It also appears by her statement to me, that her husband went off in the rebellion at the beginning, wherein he still remains. . . . The seizure must have been on some claim of confiscation, a matter of which the courts, and not the Provost-Marshals, or other military officers, are to judge—In this very case, would probably be the questions: "Is either the husband or wife a traitor?" "Does the property belong to the husband or to the wife?" "Is the property of the wife confiscable for the treason of the husband?" and other similar questions, all which it is ridiculous for a Provost-Marshal to assume to decide. The true rule for the military, is to seize such property as is needed for Military uses and reasons, and let the rest alone. Cotton and other staple articles of commerce are seizable for Military reasons; Dwelling-houses and furniture are seldom so. If Mrs. Morton is playing traitor . . . seize her, but leave her house to the courts.[37]

Even if a refugee from slavery knew that his or her master was actively supporting the Confederacy, the act did not explain how the refugee could prove this, or say who would decide whether the evidence was sufficient. By way of contrast, sections 7 and 8 of the act gave the Federal district courts jurisdiction over suits for forfeiture of other property under section 6 of the act, but no provision was made for lawsuits to establish the freedom of refugees from slavery based on section 9. "It is therefore a puzzling question," wrote J. G. Randall, "as to how, in the intention of Congress, this Confiscation Act was to be used as a measure of emancipation."[38]

Randall doubted that Congress wanted the decisions required by section 9 to be made by the military authorities. If nothing else, there was the practical problem, in a society where racially based slavery was still legal, of how the slaves emancipated by the military could prove that they were free. If their freedom had been established by the judgment of a Federal court, then this could be established by consulting court records, but no Federal court had been given jurisdiction over enforcement of section 9.

Yet military action is exactly what the language of the section suggests Congress intended. All of the slaves covered by section 9 gained their right to freedom through some interaction with the U.S. military, either by living in territory occupied by the army or by "taking refuge within the lines of the army." There was no grant of freedom to slaves who sought the protection of U.S. marshals or other civilian officials. Even more significantly, section 9 declared the slaves it freed to be "captives of war." Randall regarded this as a "rather eccentric phrase," but it echoed the military's decision during the Second Seminole War to treat as "prisoners of war" those escaped slaves who had joined Seminole Indian bands that later surrendered to the army. Determining whether specific property should be forfeited was, as Randall pointed out, a judicial decision under the U.S. Constitution. Determining who was a prisoner of war, however, had always been a matter for the military.

The Lincoln administration also saw no role for the courts in enforcing section 9. The president later instructed the attorney general to use the courts to enforce the "seizure, prosecution and condemnation" of rebel property under "the fifth, sixth and seventh sections" of the Second Confiscation Act, but made no mention of lawsuits to enforce section 9.[39] Instead, in his preliminary emancipation proclamation the president directed the military to enforce section 9. Rather than indirectly alluding to section 9, as had his initial draft emancipation proclamation, the preliminary emancipation proclamation actually issued on September 22, 1862, quoted sections 9 and 10 in full. (Section 10 prohibited return of fugitive slaves by the military.) The proclamation then ordered "all persons engaged in the military and naval service of the United States to observe, obey, and enforce, within their respective spheres of service, the act, and sections above recited."

The problem remained of how to document the fact that a person had been freed by the military under section 9, but this was not insoluble in practice. On July 17, 1863, Major General John Schofield, commanding the Department of the Missouri, requested guidance from the War Department on the military's role in implementation of the First and Second Confiscation Acts:

It is very clear to my mind that those persons declared free by the fourth section of the act of August 6, 1861, and by the ninth section of the act of July 17, 1862, are free by the operation of the law and the disloyal acts of their owners, and that no judicial decree is necessary to perfect their freedom. Is it any part of the duty of the military authorities to furnish evidence of such freedom, or must they be left to plead the acts either in suit for freedom or in defense against the person claiming their service or labor?

Judge Advocate General of the Army Joseph Holt replied that military commanders had the authority to issue the necessary papers to new freedmen:

The slaves thus enumerated, being made and declared to be captives of war as well as freedmen, are necessarily under the military control of the Government of the United States. This protection should, in good faith, be fully extended to them against all efforts made to re-enslave them or to deprive them of the freedom which this act bestows upon them. That their condition and the rights belonging to it may be known and respected, it is recommended that, through the departmental or other military commanders, certificates shall, upon a proper ascertainment of the facts, be issued to these persons, defining distinctly their status and declaring them to be, as captives of war, under the military protection of the Government. These certificates should state, briefly but distinctly, the facts on which the party's right to freedom rests, in order that it may appear the legal conclusion reached is warranted by the law as cited.[40]

In occupied Louisiana, military courts were sometimes given the task of recording emancipation under section 9.[41]

The broader significance of section 9, as applied by the Lincoln administration, was that it recognized that the freedom of an enemy's slaves could be established by military decision. The previous September, the president had asked Senator Browning whether the decision of a military commander could alter private property rights. Now Congress had determined that at least in some cases it could. In the American system of government, the main source of military authority was not to be found in acts of Congress, but rather in the president's constitutional authority to command the military to do whatever was necessary to win wars. Indirectly, the Second Confiscation Act gave the president confidence that Congress would support his constitutional authority to emancipate slaves not covered by section 9.

The most radical element in the president's initial draft, and in all succeeding versions, of the Emancipation Proclamation was its granting of freedom to slaves still in territory controlled by the Confederacy. Earlier emancipation proclamations issued by European and Latin American authorities had promised freedom to enemy slaves when, and if, they came under friendly military control, and section 9 of the Second Confiscation Act repeated this pattern. Lincoln broke completely from precedent by declaring that after January 1, 1863, "all persons held as slaves within any state or states, wherein the constitutional authority of the United States shall not then be practically recognized" would "thenceforward, and forever, be free."

Critics of Lincoln complained that because of this language the final proclamation freed not a single slave. Legal experts argued that, even under the laws of war, neither civilian courts nor military authorities could change the ownership of private property still under enemy control.[42] What the critics, both then and now, have failed to appreciate is that Lincoln was preparing to go beyond dealing with slaves as enemy property. The president would appeal to the Confederacy's slaves as people.

Senator Charles Sumner made this distinction in his main speech on the floor of the Senate in favor of the Second Confiscation Act. In preparation for this speech, the senator could rely not only on his acquaintance with the speeches of John Quincy Adams, but also on the knowledge of Dr. Francis Lieber and the research of William Whiting, later author of an influential publication defending the Confiscation Act and the Emancipation Proclamation.[43]

Sumner argued that freeing the slaves of enemies during a civil war was constitutional both as a punishment for treason and as a military measure under the laws of war. In support of the latter argument, he quoted at length from well-known works on international law by General Henry Halleck and by the Swiss jurist Emmerich de Vattel, whose works on the law of nations had been cited more than any other in the opinions of the Federal courts. "Therefore," the senator concluded, "according to the Rights of War, slaves, if property, may be declared free; or if regarded as men, they may be declared free, under two acknowledged rules: *first*, of self-interest, to procure an ally; *secondly*, of conscience and equity, to do an act of justice ennobling victory."[44]

Many of his colleagues believed that slaves were a form of private property, and Sumner was prepared to argue that the law of war allowed enemy property, including slave property, to be seized by the Federal government. The senator preferred, however, to regard slaves as persons rather than property, and argued that the enemy's slaves could be freed simply as an act of justice to the oppressed. He drew this argument from Vattel's declaration that "to deliver an oppressed people is a noble fruit of victory; it is [also] a valuable advantage gained, thus to acquire a faithful friend."[45]

The Second Confiscation Act, as finally adopted, indirectly recognized the humanity of escaped slaves by declaring them to be "captives of war," not merely enemy property. This was not enough for Sumner, who still wanted the government to expressly declare them an oppressed people, fit for liberation under Vattel's principle. When the final Emancipation Proclamation was being drafted in the fall of 1862, Sumner urged both the president and Treasury Secretary Chase to include in it a statement that emancipation was "an act of justice to an oppressed race." Chase, who was Senator Sumner's closest ally in the cabinet, eventually persuaded Lincoln to include a variant of Sumner's phrase, which declared that the proclamation was "sincerely believed to be an act of justice."[46] Chase's suggestion is usually regarded as having simply added a slight moral tone to an otherwise legalistic document. However, as an echo of Sumner's speech on the constitutional basis of the Second Confiscation Act, the phrase also gave additional legal support to the proclamation as an appeal to an oppressed people in accordance with the law of war.

8

The Proclamation as
a Weapon of War

In its final form, the Emancipation Proclamation was based on two of the government's belligerent rights under the law of war. It relied on the right to seize and destroy enemy property for reasons of military necessity, and on the right to seek allies through promising liberty to an oppressed people.

The president had decided "to procure an ally" from the enslaved people of the South months before he accepted Salmon Chase's suggestions on the wording of the final proclamation. As a military measure, the president saw emancipation primarily as a means of weakening the rebels by withdrawing slave labor from the Confederate economy and adding the labor of newly freed slaves to the Union war effort. This could only be accomplished by persuading Confederate slaves to flee their homes and seek the protection of Union military forces. As an inducement to do this, however, section 9 of the Second Confiscation Act was a seriously flawed instrument because it granted freedom only to slaves whose masters were actively supporting the rebellion, a judgment that would be made by military officers on the scene. Slaves in the Confederacy had little reason to assume that the decisions of white officers would be in their favor even if they succeeded in fleeing to a Union military camp.

This had not been a problem in earlier wars. Whether Spanish officials meeting refugees from the Carolinas in the 1690s or Royal Navy officers dealing with American slaves in 1814, military officers had previously had no reason to refuse sanctuary to anyone of African descent coming from enemy territory. In the American Civil War, however, public opinion in the North was still deeply divided on slavery in 1862, and this division was reflected in the officer corps of the army. Although a few officers ardently opposed slavery, most wanted to preserve, or at least tolerate, the South's peculiar institution. As a practical matter, the effectiveness of section 9 of the Second Confiscation Act depended on the social and political view of the officers called upon to enforce the act.

Generals with abolitionist opinions might be willing to assume, without any more evidence, that all persons fleeing from Confederate territory should benefit from section 9. More cautious or conservative officers, as well as those who feared that a massive influx of fugitives would overwhelm their resources, might be unwilling to make this assumption, and refuse aid or shelter to the refugees. In March, Congress had addressed this problem by amending the army's Articles of War to prohibit military officers from returning any fugitive slave to his or her master.[1] However, both this law and section 9 of the Second Confiscation Act could easily be circumvented by simply refusing to allow any refugees from slavery to cross U.S. military lines or enter any army camp.

At least one example of how commanders in the field could make acts of Congress ineffective had been brought to President Lincoln's attention. General Benjamin Butler, commanding the Department of the Gulf, had become the darling of antislavery activists earlier in the war when he gave refuge to fugitive slaves at Fortress Monroe in Virginia. After the government reversed the emancipation measures of General John C. Frémont and General David Hunter, General Butler decided to move in the opposite direction. In late May 1862, he ordered that no refuge be granted to fugitives from slavery in Louisiana, and directed that any refugees from slavery who had already taken shelter within U.S. military lines be expelled unless the army had work for them.[2]

The inhumanity implicit in Butler's policy became clear on June 16, after a Louisiana slave owner named LaBlanche, faced with the mounting cost of feeding his human property with no prospect of soon making any profit from their labor, apparently drove many of his slaves away from their homes and told them to seek shelter with the Union army. These displaced persons appeared before Camp Parapet and were stopped by the sentries. The officer of the day reported the situation to the camp commander, General John Phelps, as follows:

I beg leave to call your attention to the large and constantly increasing number of blacks who have congregated near the upper picket station on the river road. I learn that twenty-four hours ago they numbered about 75. The officer of the guard reports to me this morning that the number has increased to 150 or more. The first installment was sent by a man named La-blanche, from the other side of the river, in boats, on the night of the 13th, he giving them the choice, according to their statement, of leaving before sundown or receiving fifty lashes each. Many of these desire to return to their master, but are prevented by fear of harsh treatment. They are of all ages and physical condition, a number of infants in arms, many young children, robust men and women, and a large number of lame, old, and infirm of both sexes. The rest of them came in singly and in small parties from various points up the river within a hundred miles. They brought with them boxes, bedding, and luggage of all sorts, which lie strewn upon the levee and the open spaces around the picket. The women and children, and some feeble ones who needed shelter, were permitted to occupy a deserted house just outside the lines. They are quite destitute of provisions, many having eaten nothing for days except what our soldiers have given them from their own rations. In accordance with orders already issued the guard was instructed to permit none of them to enter the lines. . . . Unless supplied with the means of sustaining life by the benevolence of the military authorities or of the citizens (which is scarcely supposable) they must shortly be reduced to suffering and starvation in the very sight of the overflowing store-houses of the Government.[3]

Phelps, another Regular Army officer with abolitionist views, protested to General Butler and asked that the issue be placed before the president for decision:

Considerations of humanity are pressing for an immediate solution of their difficulties; and they are but a small portion of their race who have sought and are still seeking our pickets and our military stations, declaring that they cannot and will not any longer serve their masters, and that all they want is work and protection from us. In such a state of things the question occurs as to my own action in the case. I cannot return them to their masters, who not unfrequently come in search of them, for I am fortunately prohibited by an article of war from doing that, even if my own nature did not revolt at it; I cannot receive them, for I have neither work, shelter, nor the means . . . of making suitable arrangements with their masters until they can be provided for.[4]

Butler forwarded Phelps's request to the War Department in Washington, with a cover letter vouching for the good character of Mr. LaBlanche and claiming that, by refusing to receive fugitive slaves, Butler was merely executing government policy as he understood it. In late June, Stanton told him that the matter had been placed before the president, and that in the meantime "it has not yet . . . been deemed necessary or wise to fetter your judgment by any specific instructions in this regard."[5] Relying on this reply, Butler maintained his policy even after passage of the Second Confiscation Act.

Shortly thereafter, Lincoln sent Maryland senator Reverdy Johnson to investigate complaints that General Butler's occupation regime was arbitrary and corrupt. Ever the politician, Butler astutely deflected the investigation away from himself toward General Phelps. Johnson reported to Lincoln that the real problem was that the white people of occupied Louisiana believed the Federal government was going to free their slaves, and that the activities of General Phelps were largely responsible for this belief. Clearly irritated by the report, the president shot back a reply that, far from promising to reverse Phelps's antislavery activities, he threatened to go beyond them.

It seems the Union feeling in Louisiana is being crushed out by the course of General Phelps. Please pardon me for believing that is a false pretense. The people of Louisiana—all intelligent people everywhere—know full well, that I never had a wish to touch the foundations of their society or any right of theirs. With perfect knowledge of this, they forced a necessity upon me to send armies among them, and it is their own fault, not mine, that they are annoyed by the presence of General Phelps. They also know the remedy—know how to be cured of General Phelps. Remove the necessity of his presence. And might it not be well for them to consider whether they have not already had *time* enough to do this? If they can conceive of anything worse than General Phelps, within my power, would they not better be looking out for it? They very well know the way to avert all this is simply to take their place in the Union upon the old terms. If they will not do this, should they not receive harder blows rather than lighter ones?[6]

Unbeknownst to Butler, Phelps, and Johnson, Lincoln had already decided to inflict a harder blow on the Confederacy. Knowing the grim fate of the LaBlanche slaves, who were forced to fend for themselves in a hostile countryside after being denied access to U.S. Army posts, the president drafted his Emancipation Proclamation to reassure enslaved people who were willing to seek freedom but were reluctant to trust their future to the whims and prejudices of Federal officers like General Butler. That a refugee was fleeing from territory controlled by the Confederacy would be obvious to officers in the field. Since every fugitive coming from Confederate territory had already been declared free by the president, no discretion was left for individual officers to decide that a refugee did not legally deserve freedom. No evidence need be weighed to determine who claimed ownership of a refugee, and whether that person was a rebel. The president ordered the army to treat as free people all refugees from slavery in the Confederacy.

In modern terminology, section 9 was a weapon of economic warfare against the South, whereas the Emancipation Proclamation was a weapon of both economic and psychological warfare. The president had been told that the effectiveness of an emancipation proclamation would depend on whether it motivated an enslaved people to act. When Lincoln met with a delegation of Chicago ministers on September 13, 1862, he asked them why they thought an emancipation proclamation from the president would have more impact than section 9, which, he observed, had not "caused a single slave to come over to us." The ministers replied "that when the proclamation should become widely known (as the law of Congress has *not* been) it would withdraw the slaves from the rebels, leaving them without laborers, and giving us *both laborers and soldiers.*"[7] A presidential proclamation would achieve a notoriety that an obscure section of an act of Congress would not, and consequently would have a greater psychological impact.

By declaring that the Federal government recognized the present freedom of all persons enslaved in the Confederacy, the Emancipation Proclamation made it clear that anyone who worked or fought for the Union was also working and fighting to bring freedom to every slave still in rebel territory as of January 1, 1863. A refugee could, in good conscience, flee to Union forces in the belief that he or she would be given a chance to work toward the freedom of loved ones left behind. By recognizing the freedom of a subject people, Lincoln was striking at the power of the Confederate government in much the same way that France had struck at the power of the British government in 1778 by recognizing the United States as an independent nation. The Confederates had hoped for similar support from Britain and France for its own independence. Now Lincoln had turned the recognition weapon against them by declaring that his government would "recognize and maintain the freedom" of the Confederacy's oppressed minority.

Lincoln's decision to recognize the immediate freedom of all enslaved persons in the Confederacy was, and still is, derided as a futile act with little or no practical effect. From the point of view of individuals, held in bondage deep behind Confederate lines, this was quite true. However, its potential impact on the war would be immediate and vast. It would make a negotiated settlement, based on the South's return to the Union as it was in 1860, virtually impossible.

In mid-1862, the U.S. government still agreed with the Confederate government that slavery was a legitimate institution in those states that had it, and that the Federal government was obligated under the Constitution to help return fugitives from bondage to their owners. In principle, this was true even of slaves held in areas in rebellion against the United States.

The Emancipation Proclamation ended this commonality of views. As of January 1, 1863, the official position of the Federal government (or at least that part of the government Lincoln controlled) was that thousands of free persons were being illegally held in bondage in the seceded states. Any negotiation seeking the return of these states to the Union would have to grapple with the future status of these people. If the Emancipation Proclamation had followed historic precedent, or merely conformed to the strict terms of the Second Confiscation Act, a negotiated settlement would have been somewhat more difficult, but not impossible. The Federal government could still have insisted that the relatively few refugees who had escaped to Union military lines must remain free, and there was at least some chance that the Confederate authorities would have agreed, perhaps in exchange for monetary compensation to their owners as the American and British governments had agreed after the War of 1812. After January 1, 1863, however, the

United States would insist that, as a condition of peace, the South recognize the freedom of hundreds of thousands of slaves who had never been near a single Federal soldier. These were the truly radical implications of Lincoln's draft emancipation proclamation.

The preliminary emancipation proclamation of September 1862, and the final proclamation signed in January 1863, retained the essential features of the president's initial draft—citing both the power of the commander in chief and the will of Congress as legal foundations for the act, a presidential finding of military necessity, and freedom for all who were in enslaved in enemy territory. The preliminary proclamation reinforced the initial draft's implied assertion that the president was executing the will of Congress by quoting the entire text of sections 9 and 10 of the Second Confiscation Act, as well as the new Article of War prohibiting the return of fugitive slaves by the military. The final proclamation retreated slightly from the initial draft and the interim proclamation by declaring the affected slaves to be "free," rather than "forever free." This probably reflected the president's continuing doubt that the Federal courts would uphold the proclamation, together with his reluctance to promise an oppressed people more than he was sure he could deliver.[8]

The most startling difference between the final proclamation and its predecessors was the president's announcement that slaves freed under it "will be received into the armed service of the United States to garrison forts, positions, stations, and other places, and to man vessels of all sorts in said service."[9] Traditionally, enemy slaves freed during wartime had been actively recruited to fight against their former masters. During the American Revolution, the royal governor of Virginia raised an "Ethiopian Regiment" from the slaves of the rebellious colonists, and during the War of 1812 the Royal Navy enlisted slaves of American masters into the "Royal Colonial Marines." In his emancipation proclamation, Simon Bolivar required healthy males to serve in the war against Spain as a condition for the freedom of their families.

President Lincoln was at first reluctant to use former slaves as soldiers, even though Congress had amended the Militia Act to allow this. When the issue was raised at the cabinet meeting on July 22, the president opposed enlisting black troops, but by the end of the meeting Secretary Chase had the impression that he would not object to arming for self-defense black workers hired by the army.

As a general proposition, President Lincoln knew that the Union needed more soldiers, but he was getting conflicting military advice from his field commanders on whether the army should recruit liberated slaves. Whereas General Hunter, in the Department of the South, insisted he needed to form colored military units, General Butler, in the Department of the Gulf, was certain that former slaves would be ineffective as soldiers. Conservative politicians and newspapers further claimed that many white soldiers would throw down their arms rather than fight alongside black units.[10]

The potential for raising Confederate morale was a major concern. Having decided in favor of a bold use of emancipation as an offensive weapon, Lincoln was reluctant to further alienate Southern opinion by arming and organizing slaves to fight against their former masters. Throughout 1861, the president had clung to the hope that white Southerners would come to their senses, reject the leadership of die-hard secessionists, and return to the Union. These hopes had weakened almost to the point of extinction after the battle of Shiloh and General George McClellan's defeat in the Peninsula, but they still had enough residual strength to keep the president from immediately backing the enlistment of African Americans in July.

Pressure from military officers in the field eventually tipped the balance in favor of enlisting refugees from slavery. General David Hunter had doggedly continued to seek official approval for his program to recruit black soldiers. On July 11, he wrote the secretary of war to "most earnestly beg that by return of mail you will give me full authority to muster into the service of the United States, as infantry, all loyal men to be found in my department, and that I be authorized to appoint all the officers." As both he and Stanton knew, the phrase "all loyal men" was a code for enlisting soldiers without regard to race. "This," he emphasized, "has now become a military necessity in this department."[11] Hunter received no answer.

On July 15, however, Congress passed an amendment to the Militia Act authorizing the enlistment of African American soldiers.[12] Encouraged by the new law, General Hunter tried again on August 4. He announced to the War Department that he had raised a colored regiment, the First South Carolina Volunteers, and requested authority to appoint officers for it.[13] Again, there was no reply from Washington. Exasperated, on August 10 General Hunter reported that "failing to receive authority to muster the First Regiment of South Carolina Volunteers into the service of the United States, I have disbanded them."[14]

In occupied Louisiana, passage of the Militia Act amendment had inspired General Phelps to raise five companies of African American soldiers. General Butler, however, refused to issue them arms and equipment, and ordered that they be employed as civilian laborers rather than soldiers. Phelps had had enough, and he resigned his commission.[15]

Phelps's resignation and Hunter's threat to dissolve the First South Carolina Volunteers seem finally to have moved the president to make a firm decision, and he decided in favor of enlisting soldiers "of African descent." On August 25, the Commanding General of the Army wrote to General Rufus Saxton, who had been appointed by the War Department to handle refugee affairs in the Department of the South, that he now had the authority "to arm, uniform, equip, and receive into the service of the United States such number of volunteers of African descent as you may deem expedient, not exceeding 50,000," and to "detail officers to instruct them in military drill, discipline, and duty, and to command them."[16]

Once he had decided to offer freedom to enemy slaves and to arm those who responded, Lincoln firmly and persistently backed both policies. In March he urged Andrew Johnson, the military governor of Tennessee, "and himself a slave holder," to raise black regiments for duty in the West. "The bare sight of fifty thousand armed, and drilled, black soldiers on the banks of the Mississippi," wrote the president, "would end the rebellion at once."[17]

General Hunter must have felt vindicated when he received a letter from the president praising the performance of the First and Second South Carolina Volunteers in Florida. "I see the enemy are driving at them fiercely," the president wrote. "It is important to the enemy that such a force shall *not* take shape, and grow, and thrive, in the South; and in precisely the same proportion it is important to us that it *shall*."[18] In December 1863, acceptance of the Emancipation Proclamation was made an express condition for presidential amnesty for individual Confederates, and Lincoln told Congress he would never retract the proclamation. "If the people should, by whatever mode or means, make it an Executive duty to re-enslave" persons freed by the proclamation, "another, and not I, must be their instrument," he later declared.[19]

He seems to have wavered only once. In the summer of 1864, the war appeared to have arrived at a bloody stalemate. In the run-up to the fall presidential election, critics charged that Lincoln's insistence on preserving the Emancipation Proclamation was preventing peace negotiations that could reunify the country. In August, the president composed a letter to Charles Robinson, a Democratic editor, defending the contribution of black soldiers to the war effort and the need to enforce the proclamation's promise of freedom. At the very end of the letter, however, he added, "if Jefferson Davis wishes, for himself, or for the benefit of his friends at the North, to know what I would do if he were to offer peace and re-union, saying nothing about slavery, let him try me."[20] This draft was written at a time when Lincoln believed he would lose the November election. Five days later he wrote the so-called blind memorandum, which outlined his plans for the rest of his term of office if his opponent, George B. McClellan, was elected president: "This morning, as for some days past, it seems exceedingly probable that this Administration will not be re-elected. Then it will be my duty to so co-operate with the President elect, as to save the Union between the election and the inauguration; as he will have secured his election on such ground that he can not possibly save it afterwards."[21]

McClellan had always disagreed with the Emancipation Proclamation, and if he became president that document would be either withdrawn or ignored. In August 1864, believing that the proclamation was already doomed to failure, Lincoln might well have considered peace negotiations without regard to the future of slavery. If the president did entertain these doubts, he soon abandoned them. The letter to Charles Robinson was never sent.

The Proclamation as Permanent Policy

The Confederate response to the September 1862 preliminary emancipation proclamation came on December 23, 1862, in the form of a counter-proclamation from Jefferson Davis.[22] Lincoln's preliminary proclamation had placed Davis in a quandary. He could hardly protest that the proclamation violated Southern state rights under the Constitution because that would concede that the Confederate states were still in the Union, just as Lincoln contended. If the Confederacy was what it claimed to be—an independent nation at war with another nation—it had little basis upon which to object to the Emancipation Proclamation. The wartime practice of offering freedom to an enemy's slaves had become too common and well known.

The president of the Confederacy therefore shifted his aim, attacking the proclamation as an effort to incite slaves to revolt and murder white civilians. In the preliminary proclamation, Lincoln had stated that "the executive government of the United States, including the military and naval authority thereof, will recognize and maintain the freedom" of anyone freed by the final proclamation, and "will do no act or acts to repress such persons, or any of them, in any efforts they may make for their actual freedom." Davis charged that this language, by declaring that the United States would do nothing to suppress a slave insurrection, no matter how bloody it became, was a direct incitement for slaves to attack their masters indiscriminately.

By making this charge, Davis was attempting some psychological warfare of his own, appealing both to Northern conservatives and to public opinion in Europe. In England and France, concern had been widely expressed that the Emancipation Proclamation would incite an indiscriminate race war. The head of the British mission in Washington even advised his government that the preliminary proclamation was a "cold, vindictive" act with no "pretext of humanity," and that it offered "direct encouragement to servile insurrections."[23] On the advice of Secretary of State William Seward and Treasury Secretary Salmon Chase, Lincoln omitted the offending language from the final Emancipation Proclamation and added an injunction "upon the people so declared to be free to abstain from all violence," unless in self-defense.[24]

Having charged the Lincoln administration with waging indiscriminate warfare against Southern whites, Davis ordered retaliation. Black soldiers captured by Confederate forces would not be considered prisoners of war, but treated as fugitive slaves; any not claimed by a master would be sold. Captured white officers of black soldiers would be turned over to state authorities to be prosecuted for inciting slave rebellion. In the end, Confederate forces in the field never pursued a consistent policy when they captured African American Union soldiers. Some were sold as slaves, but others were sent to prison camps such as Andersonville, like white prisoners of war. When their officers were not around, Confederate soldiers often simply refused to accept the surrender of black soldiers and killed them on the field of battle.

Davis's order had an immediate effect on one project of the U.S. War Department. During the Civil War, thousands of army officers had been appointed directly from civilian life. Unlike the professional officers of the small Regular Army, these men usually knew nothing about the laws and customs of war. To remedy this defect, on December

17, 1862, a committee was appointed to draft an official codification of the laws of war for the guidance of the army. The only civilian on the committee was its chairman, Dr. Francis Lieber of Columbia College, a friend of General in Chief Henry Halleck and the most eminent American expert on the law of war in the mid-nineteenth century. The code the committee produced was issued in April 1863 as Army General Order 100. Historians generally agree that it was primarily drafted by Lieber, with little or no input from the other members.

Francis Lieber was a man of contradictions. Although he rejected the label "abolitionist," Dr. Lieber opposed slavery and "encouraged and advised" Senator Charles Sumner's attacks on the institution in Congress.[25] He had taught in both New York City and Charleston, South Carolina, and had sons in both the Union and Confederate armies. Although he had criticized General Hunter's emancipation decree on technical legal grounds, he strongly agreed with Hunter that the modern law of war (or "martial law") was incompatible with slavery. According to his chief biographer, when Lieber was appointed to codify the laws of war for the U.S. Army, one of his objectives was "to lay down a clear-cut army rule based on international law which would free the Negroes of seceded states as they came within the jurisdiction of the Union army."[26] For Dr. Lieber, the law of war was based on natural law, which treated all persons as equals. Slavery was inconsistent with natural law, and it could only exist as a part of the local, or "municipal," law of individual states or nations. He concluded that during war, any slave escaping to territory controlled by the enemy army automatically became free, because relations between enemies were governed solely by the law of war.

Jefferson Davis's order that black Union soldiers be treated as escaped slaves was a direct affront to Francis Lieber's understanding of a law of war based on natural law. Because natural law regarded all human beings as equal, there could be no lawful discrimination against some prisoners of war based on their race.

Under Lieber's influence, this erudite legal theorizing became official policy of the U.S. Army. His codification of the law of war in General Order 100 included articles directly challenging Jefferson Davis's retaliation order:

Article 40. There exists no law or body of authoritative rules of action between hostile armies, except that branch of the law of nature and nations which is called the law and usages of war on land.

. . . .

Article 42. Slavery, complicating and confounding the ideas of property, (that is of a thing,) and of personality, (that is of humanity,) exists according to municipal or local law only. The law of nature and nations has never acknowledged it. The digest of the Roman law enacts the early dictum of the pagan jurist, that "so far as the law of nature is concerned, all men are equal." Fugitives escaping from a country in which they were slaves, villains, or serfs, into another country, have, for centuries past, been held free and acknowledged free by judicial decisions of European countries, even though the municipal law of the country in which the slave had taken refuge acknowledged slavery within its own dominions.

Article 43. Therefore, in a war between the United States and a belligerent which admits of slavery, if a person held in bondage by that belligerent be captured by or come as a fugitive under the protection of the military forces of the United States, such person is immediately entitled to the rights and privileges of a freeman. To return such person into slavery would amount to enslaving a free person, and neither the United States nor any officer under their authority can enslave any human being.

. . . .

Article 57. . . . No belligerent has a right to declare that enemies of a certain class, color, or condition, when properly organized as soldiers, will not be treated by him as public enemies [and as prisoners of war when captured].

Article 58. The law of nations knows of no distinction of color, and if an enemy of the United States should enslave and sell any captured persons of their army, it would be a case for the severest retaliation, if not redressed upon complaint. The United States cannot retaliate by enslavement; therefore death must be the retaliation for this crime against the law of nations.[27]

During the Civil War, Army General Orders were usually issued under the authority of the General in Chief of the Army or the secretary of war. General Order 100 of 1863, however, was personally approved by

President Lincoln as commander in chief. It remained the official army guidance on the laws of war and military occupation until well into the twentieth century.

Only four months after signing his final Emancipation Proclamation on January 1, 1863, President Lincoln, following the advice of Dr. Lieber and the example of General Hunter, had insured that no future president would have to issue such a proclamation ever again. In 1846–1847, the United States' conquest of New Mexico, Arizona, and California meant that slavery might be re-introduced into an area where the Mexican government had abolished it. In contrast, after General Order 100, whenever the U.S. Army marched into enemy territory in a future war any persons there held as slaves would be freed. Now freedom would follow the flag.

The International Impact

Shortly before General Order 100 was issued, the U.S. government received the first indications that the South was prepared to enforce Jefferson Davis's order. Officials of Massachusetts heard a report that two black servants of one of their officers had been sold in Texas. (To add to the irony of the situation, one of the men was the grandson of a black veteran of the Revolutionary War.) Secretary of War Edwin Stanton referred the matter to the U.S. commissary for exchange of prisoners, Major General Ethan Allen Hitchcock, who correctly predicted that raising the matter with his Confederate counterpart would only be met with insults.[28] Since the Confederate authorities refused to cooperate, later efforts to verify or refute reported incidents of abuse of black prisoners were similarly inconclusive.[29]

The Confederate government wanted to discourage the raising of black soldiers by the Federal government, and similar practices in the twentieth century suggest that its refusal to comment either way on the treatment, or existence, of black prisoners may have been part of this policy. During World War II, Hitler tried to terrorize resistance movements in occupied Europe by issuing his "Night and Fog Decree," under which suspects would be quietly arrested in the middle of the night and never heard of again. Their friends and relatives had no way of learning whether they were alive or dead, free or in a concentration camp. Many authoritarian governments have since adopted similar practices, so that opponents simply "disappear." The Confederacy's policy of neither confirming nor denying that they held captured black soldiers may also have been intended to terrorize potential recruits to the Union army.

In light of Jefferson Davis's order and the confusion about whether it was being enforced, Senator Charles Sumner asked the president at the end of May 1864 to issue a proclamation formally declaring that the United States would insist that colored soldiers be treated as prisoners of war, and threatening retaliation if the enemy did not comply.[30] Lincoln responded on July 30, publicly reaffirming and personally endorsing the nondiscrimination policies adopted in General Order 100:

> It is the duty of every Government to give protection to its citizens, of whatsoever class, color, or condition, and especially to those who are duly organized as soldiers in the public service. The law of nations and the usages and customs of war, as carried on by civilized powers, permit no distinction as to color in the treatment of prisoners of war as public enemies. To sell or enslave any captured person on account of his color and for no offense against the laws of war is a relapse into barbarism and a crime against the civilization of the age.
>
> The Government of the United States will give the same protection to all its soldiers; and if the enemy shall sell or enslave any one because of his color, the offense shall be punished by retaliation upon the enemy's prisoners in our possession.[31]

Lincoln never carried out this threat of retaliation because he found it morally repugnant to punish the innocent for the offenses of another. He did, however, refuse amnesty to Confederates who refused to treat African Americans as prisoners of war, with the clear implication they would be prosecuted after the end of the war.[32] More significantly, he ordered an end to the exchange of prisoners of war so long as the South refused to include black prisoners in those exchanges.[33]

As an act of moral courage, the decision to suspend exchanges ranks with the Emancipation Proclamation and with Lincoln's unpopular decision to grant clemency to 300 Indian warriors condemned to death in 1862. White prisoners of war resented losing their best chance for freedom merely to protect black prisoners, and their relatives were almost certain to reflect this resentment at the polls. The president nevertheless maintained this policy until the Confederates capitulated and agreed to exchange black soldiers in early 1865.

General Order 100 provided the standard guidance on the law of war to the army well into the twentieth century, but its impact was felt long afterward and far outside the United States. In translation, it was adopted by many European armies and formed the basis for the first international codification of the law of war by the 1899 Hague Peace Conference. Even during the height of European imperialism, when many intellectuals defended the superiority of the white race, the Lieber Code remained an authoritative reminder that the international law of war recognized no distinction between races. Its spirit is reflected in the 1949 Geneva Convention on Prisoners of War, which states that "all prisoners of war shall be treated alike by the Detaining Power, without any adverse distinction based on race, nationality, religious belief or political opinions, or any other distinction founded on similar criteria."[34] The Lieber Code's rules on slavery and racial discrimination, which resulted directly from the Emancipation Proclamation, are one of the foundations of the modern law of war and international human rights law.

9

The Conkling Letter

Whatever its long-term international effects, General Order 100 had no discernable impact on the political and legal debate about the morality, wisdom, and constitutionality of the Emancipation Proclamation. This intense, emotional, and highly learned controversy began as soon as the preliminary proclamation was issued and continued after the final proclamation entered into force.[1] The president initially remained aloof from the furor he had provoked, waiting for the right time and occasion before publicly defending this most controversial of his actions.

One important development came on March 10, 1863, when the U.S. Supreme Court issued its decision in *The Prize Cases*.[2] Several neutral merchant ships had been captured by the U.S. Navy while attempting to evade the blockade on Confederate ports. The navy placed prize crews aboard these vessels and sailed them to Northern ports to be condemned, along with their cargos, as prizes of war by U.S. district courts. The owners contested the legality of the captures, arguing that although blockading an enemy's coast was authorized by the laws of war, no international war, declared by Congress, existed, and that in any event it was Congress, not the president, that had to authorize a blockade. Eventually these cases came before the Supreme Court of the United States, and that Court upheld the president's power to apply the law of war:

> The parties . . . in a public war are independent nations. But it is not necessary to constitute war, that both parties should be acknowledged as independent nations or sovereign States. A war may exist where one of the belligerents, claims sovereign rights as against the other.
>
> . . . .
>
> It is not the less a civil war, with belligerent parties in hostile array, because it be called an "insurrection" by one side, and

133

the insurgents be considered as rebels or traitors. It is not necessary that the independence of the revolted province or State be
acknowledged in order to constitute it a party belligerent in a
war according to the law of nations. . . .

Whether the President in fulfilling his duties, as Commander-
in-Chief, in suppressing an insurrection, has met with such
armed hostile resistance, and a civil war of such alarming proportions as will compel him to accord to them the character of belligerents, is a question to be decided by him, and this Court must
be governed by the decisions and acts of the political department
of the Government to which this power was entrusted. . . . The
proclamation of blockade is itself official and conclusive evidence
to the Court that a state of war existed which demanded and
authorized a recourse to such a measure, under the circumstances
peculiar to the case. . . .

We are of the opinion that the President had a right, *jure
belli* [by the law of war], to institute a blockade of ports in possession of the States in rebellion, which neutrals are bound to
regard.

Chief Justice Taney and three of his colleagues dissented.

The Supreme Court had finally ruled that a true war existed, and
that the president could rely on the international law of war to define
his power as commander in chief. No longer was there a need to equiv-
ocate, as he had in the Emancipation Proclamation, over the nature
and sources of his power to fight the war with the weapons he deemed
best.

On June 17, 1863, Lincoln's opponents held a mass meeting in
Springfield, Illinois, where the speakers denounced the Emancipation
Proclamation and the enlistment of black soldiers, and demanded an
immediate end to the war.[3] To counter this demonstration, Illinois Republicans organized their own mass meeting.

On August 14, Republican leader James C. Conkling invited the
president to speak to "a Grand Mass Meeting at Springfield on the
3rd day of September."[4] The meeting would be open to "unconditional
Union men of all parties," so the audience would include conservative
Republicans and War Democrats who doubted both the legality and the
wisdom of the Emancipation Proclamation. In late summer 1863, the
Army of the Potomac was still recovering from the battle of Gettysburg,

while Lincoln was urging General George Meade to follow up his victory there by attacking Lee's army. Understandably, the president was unable to attend the Springfield meeting.

Despite his inability to appear in person, the president decided to use the occasion to draft a definitive military, political, and legal defense of his Emancipation Policy, to be read to the meeting. He had been gathering material and making notes for a reply to his critics for some time, and on August 23 he brought these resources together at the White House and began work on the letter. One witness remembered him working at a table strewn with "a variety of newspapers, rolled-up maps and assorted odds and ends of letters and orders."[5] By August 26, he was finished, and sent the result back to James Conkling. After being read to an enthusiastic crowd of more than 50,000 at the fairground in Springfield, the letter was widely praised in the press and reprinted by the Republican Party for the fall elections. Historians credit it with having an important effect on the state elections of 1863.[6]

Lincoln devoted most of the Conkling letter to demonstrating the military importance of emancipation and the use of black troops, and explaining why, in the current circumstances, peace negotiations would be futile. Now that the Supreme Court had freed him to rely openly on the law of war, Lincoln could cut through the constitutional objections to the Emancipation Proclamation with a few sentences of hard, sharp logic:

> You dislike the emancipation proclamation; and, perhaps would have it retracted—You say it is unconstitutional—I think differently. I think the constitution invests its commander-in-chief, with the law of war in time of war—The most that can be said, if so much, is that slaves are property. Is there—has there ever been—any question that by the law of war, property, both of enemies and friends, may be taken when needed? And is it not needed whenever taking it, helps us, or hurts the enemy? Armies, the world over, destroy enemies' property when they can not use it; and even destroy their own to keep it from the enemy. Civilized belligerents do all in their power to help themselves, or hurt the enemy, except a few things regarded as barbarous or cruel. Among the exceptions are the massacre of vanquished foes, and non-combatants, male and female.[7]

The principal arguments, and some of the language, in this paragraph were derived from Orville H. Browning's September 30, 1861, letter citing Jean Jacques Burlamaqui in defense of General Frémont's emancipation order. To defend the Emancipation Proclamation to a conservative Illinois audience, it was natural for Lincoln to turn to the letter from his conservative Illinois friend. (Ironically, by 1863 Browning had changed his position and become a critic of the proclamation.)

The key ideas in this paragraph of the Conkling letter—the relationship of the Constitution to the law of war; the legitimacy, under the law of war, of almost any means of hurting the enemy; and destruction of private property as one of those means—closely parallel the arguments in Browning's letter. By itself, this does not necessarily establish any direct connection between the two documents. By the middle of 1863, many defenders of military emancipation were also expressing these ideas. A comprehensive treatment of these arguments had been published by William Whiting, the solicitor of the War Department, in his pamphlet *War Powers of the President and Congress*. In the Senate, Charles Sumner had eloquently defended emancipation under the war powers.

However, there is other, more convincing, evidence of a direct connection between the 1863 letter to Conkling and the 1861 letter from Browning. Two phrases appear in both documents, and nowhere else in Lincoln's writings. An online search of the Lincoln papers in the Library of Congress found no document, other than the Conkling letter, where the president used the phrase "is there any question that" something is true. This phrase was simply not part of Lincoln's rhetorical toolkit. In his September 30, 1861, letter, however, Browning had used the phrase "is there any question" in referring to the positive effect of Frémont's proclamation. In both letters, the phrase is used in a rhetorical question to make the point that whatever harms the enemy is legitimate in war. In picking up the idea, Lincoln also retained the phrase.

The other phrase Lincoln used only in the Conkling letter is "barbarous or cruel." Indeed, another online search of the Lincoln papers found that nowhere else does Lincoln use even the word "barbarous." However, a very similar phrase does appear in the writings of Burlamaqui. With regard to the enemy's "old men, women, and children," he writes, it would be "a barbarous cruelty" to kill them.[8] Lincoln and Burlamaqui use these similar phrases to make essentially the same point—that the deliberate killing of noncombatants is prohibited even in war. In using an idea from another source, Lincoln again retained and adapted the way it was expressed.

Burlamaqui's reference to "barbarous cruelty" was not among the quotations Browning included in his September 30, 1861, letter to Lincoln. When drafting the Conkling letter, it appears that Lincoln not only reread Browning's letter, but, like any good lawyer, directly consulted the authority Browning had cited—Jean Jacques Burlamaqui, as translated by Thomas Nugent.

Using these resources, Lincoln compressed a complex and sophisticated legal argument into one short paragraph defending the legality of the Emancipation Proclamation. He began by asserting that as commander in chief he had been invested with "the law of war, in time of war," reminding his audience of the Supreme Court's recent decision to that effect in *The Prize Cases*. His argument then reverses course, appearing to concede to his critics the most conservative position on the law of American slavery—that slaves were property and nothing more than property; that the only human rights involved in slavery were the slave owners' property rights. But even if these propositions were true, Lincoln replies, the law of war allows the president to infringe on property rights by "taking" them for valid military reasons, and those reasons include any act that "helps us, or hurts the enemy."

Political conservatives have always valued tradition, custom, and precedent, so Lincoln next invokes historical precedent for his taking of property by the Emancipation Proclamation. "Armies, the world over, destroy enemies' property when they can not use it; and even destroy their own to keep it from the enemy." In his address to the Cooper Institute in 1860, Lincoln defended the Republican position that Congress could keep slavery from spreading to new territories by showing that a majority of the Founders of the Republic had shared this interpretation of the Constitution. "What is conservatism?" he then asked. "Is it not adherence to the old and tried, against the new and untried?"[9] Just as he had claimed the mantle of conservatism for the Republican Party in 1860, so in 1863 he claimed that the Emancipation Proclamation had a traditional, and therefore conservative, foundation in the law of war.

Tradition could only take Lincoln so far, however, because he had tried to do something that no other military commander ever had—the Emancipation Proclamation purported to "take" enemy property that was not yet under his control. No traditional practice supported that, as his critics pointed out.

In the next sentence of the Conkling letter, Lincoln therefore altered the direction of his legal argument. Instead of historical precedents, he now turned to the fundamental legal principles that Burlamaqui had expounded. "Civilized belligerents do *all in their power* to help themselves, or hurt the enemy, except a few things regarded as barbarous or cruel." (Emphasis added.) Here Lincoln invoked what some have referred to as the "prohibitory" character of the law of war—that is, whatever is not prohibited by that law is permitted in war. Under this principle, any measure that will hurt the enemy is lawful, unless some specific rule of law forbids it, such as the rule Lincoln cited against the "massacre of vanquished foes, and non-combatants." That there were no historical precedents for taking property, or freeing slaves, still under enemy control was unimportant. These actions were legal unless Lincoln's opponents could point to a rule of law that prohibited them.

The final sentence, referring to the prohibition against killing prisoners of war or noncombatants, seems out of place. This rule had little to do with justifying the Emancipation Proclamation, the overall purpose of this paragraph of the Conkling letter. Several possible reasons might be suggested. Confederate authorities had criticized the Lieber Code, General Order 100, that Lincoln had signed in April, charging that it authorized unrestrained violence under the principle of military necessity. They had earlier charged that the Emancipation Proclamation itself was intended to incite slave revolts that would lead to the massacre of white women and children. Lincoln probably wanted to refute these allegations and reaffirm that his administration valued the customary limits on violence established by the law of war.

He was also concerned about the fate of black soldiers who had "disappeared" after capture by enemy forces, especially in light of Confederate threats to refuse them prisoner of war status. It would not hurt to remind the South that the United States would regard any "massacre" of its soldiers as a serious violation of the law of war.

10

A Radical Recognition
of Freedom

In a lecture at the Lincoln Museum in 2004, Allen Guelzo noted that "the most obvious fact about the Emancipation Proclamation that raises question-marks in people's minds is the matter of timing: *why did he wait so long?* . . . If the Civil War was really about slavery, and Lincoln was in earnest about abolishing slavery, why didn't he pick up his pen on April 13th, 1861, [when Fort Sumter surrendered] and free the Confederacy's slaves *then?*"[1] During his lifetime, Lincoln's antislavery critics had faulted him for delaying almost two years before issuing an emancipation proclamation. "From the genuine abolition ground," Frederick Douglass observed in 1876, "Mr. Lincoln seemed tardy, cold, dull and indifferent." In the twentieth century, this complaint was taken up by some activists for civil rights and racial equality.[2]

These critics have a point. By 1861, it had become a common practice for governments at war with a slave-holding enemy to offer freedom to their adversary's slaves. Why didn't President Lincoln use this weapon against the South from the day the Confederates fired on Fort Sumter, just as he authorized the army to use muskets and cannon, and the navy to impose a blockade? At the beginning, the president must have hoped that, like President Washington in the Whiskey Rebellion, he could face down the secessionists without resorting to a full-scale war. By September, however, it was clear that the government would have to accord the Confederates most, if not all, the rights and privileges of a belligerent power under the international law of war. Lincoln's correspondence with Senator Orville Browning about John C. Frémont's emancipation order indicates that the president had already decided on the legal test—military necessity—that he would eventually use to justify the Emancipation Proclamation. If the Confederates were to be given rights under the law of war, why shouldn't they suffer the penalties of that law as well, including having their slaves freed by the enemy army?

Professor Guelzo and others have pointed out that in the fall and winter of 1861, there was in fact a military necessity *not* to emancipate the enemy's slaves, because this would have caused the secession of Kentucky, a strategically important border state. That necessity had ended by March 1862, however, and still the president waited. He waited until General McClellan's army had been thrown back from the gates of Richmond, and the need for new approaches to the war were obvious. Only then, after the military necessity for emancipation would be clear to all but die-hard supporters of slavery, did he tell his cabinet that he had decided to issue an emancipation proclamation.

In the eyes of Lincoln's critics, his delay can only be attributed to racism and a secret sympathy for the institution of slavery. The president's qualms about the legality of emancipation, as expressed in his letters to Senator Browning, can be dismissed as excessive sensitivity to the constitutional rights of slaveholders, combined with callousness toward the victims of slavery.

The unspoken assumptions of these critics are that any emancipation proclamation, even an unconstitutional one, was better than none at all, and that the president would have acted on that basis if he truly hated slavery. An invalid emancipation proclamation could do no harm, they assume, and might do some good by encouraging slaves to seek freedom. Even if the courts overturned the proclamation, at least some of these refugees would escape and remain free. As "Black power" advocate Julius Lester wrote in 1968, "his pen was sitting on his desk the whole time. All he had to do was get up one morning and say 'Doggonit! I think I gon free the slaves today. It just ain't right for folks to own other folks.' It was that simple."

Under nineteenth-century American law, however, it was not that simple. Then, as now, officers of the U.S. Army swore an oath to preserve, protect, and defend the Constitution, which declared the president to be their commander in chief. President Lincoln had a duty to the officers who had taken that oath not to order them to perform acts that he knew the courts would find to be illegal.

As a lawyer, Lincoln also knew that Federal officers who loyally carried out his illegal orders could be held personally liable for any monetary damages that resulted. Officers who received and protected fugitives under an illegal emancipation proclamation could be successfully sued by the aggrieved slave owners. Chief Justice Taney had already ruled that superior orders provided no defense for an officer who took an American citizen's property. It was unlikely that Taney and his colleagues would make an exception for the antislavery orders of a president many of them loathed.

If the issue reached the Federal courts they might well hold that there was no true military necessity, and therefore no legal justification, for a premature emancipation proclamation. By waiting until the military necessity for emancipation was palpable and obvious, President Lincoln greatly increased the chances that his Emancipation Proclamation would be upheld by the courts, and that loyal officers would not suffer for obeying it. The legal context in which he waged the war, rather than reluctance to strike at slavery, is a more likely explanation for why the president waited to issue his Emancipation Proclamation.

If Lincoln was really a reluctant emancipator who secretly believed in slavery, it is difficult to understand why the proclamation he issued was so radical in its scope. Had the proclamation truly been issued reluctantly, in response to abolitionist and Radical Republican pressure, then it should have gone no further than the other military emancipation documents issued in the eighteenth and nineteenth centuries, and granted freedom only to refugees who actually escaped to Union military lines. Section 9 of the Second Confiscation Act, which Lincoln quoted in his preliminary proclamation, only went this far, and the president could easily have deferred to Congress if he was acting only in response to pressure and against his personal inclinations.

Both section 9 and the historical precedents were based on the laws governing enemy property in wartime, and one cannot seize enemy property unless one has control of it. Lincoln, however, drafted his proclamation to emphatically reject the idea that it was limited by the rules applicable to property. From the speeches of Senator Sumner, his correspondence with Senator Browning, and other sources, the president had learned that the law of war permitted him to do anything to defeat an enemy, except for a few acts that were inhumane. By declaring that the U.S. government immediately recognized the freedom of all slaves in the Confederacy, Lincoln dealt with them as an oppressed people, rather than as property, and appealed for their support as humans.

The document Lincoln signed on January 1, 1863, was the last emancipation proclamation issued in Western military history. Slavery was still legal in Brazil and the Spanish colonies of the Caribbean, but the death of the institution in the United States doomed it throughout the Western hemisphere.

Despite the end of slavery, the Emancipation Proclamation remains an important precedent. As an official refusal to recognize the legitimacy of enslaving a whole people, and an encouragement for them to resist, the Emancipation Proclamation found many echoes in the conflicts of the twentieth century. In 1932, for example, Secretary of State Henry Stimson declared that the United States would not recognize any territorial changes resulting from Japanese aggression against China. The United States and other Western governments refused to recognize Stalin's annexation of the Baltic Republics of Latvia, Lithuania, and Estonia in 1940, a policy that aided their recovery of independence in 1991. During World War II, neither the United States nor the United Kingdom recognized the Vichy regime in France, and both gave material aid to the Free French forces that continued to resist German occupation. These policies attained universal approval in 1974, when the United Nations General Assembly adopted a definition of aggression that declared: "No territorial acquisition or special advantage resulting from aggression is or shall be recognized as lawful."[3]

Many other examples could be given. What is significant is that Lincoln's decision to recognize the freedom of an oppressed people, to offer them assistance in securing that freedom, and to ask their aid against a common enemy, has remained an important diplomatic weapon in the continuing struggle for human liberty.

Appendix A

First Confiscation Act,
August 6, 1861

CHAP. LX.—*An Act to confiscate Property
used for Insurrectionary Purposes.*

*Be it enacted by the Senate and House of Representatives of the United
States of America in Congress assembled,* That if, during the present or
any future insurrection against the Government of the United States,
after the President of the United States shall have declared, by proclamation, that the laws of the United States are opposed, and the
execution thereof obstructed, by combinations too powerful to be suppressed by the ordinary course of judicial proceedings, or by the power
vested in the marshals by law, any person or persons, his, her, or their
agent, attorney, or employee, shall purchase or acquire, sell or give,
any property of whatsoever kind or description, with intent to use or
employ the same, or suffer the same to be used or employed, in aiding,
abetting, or promoting such insurrection or resistance to the laws, or
any person or persons engaged therein; or if any person or persons,
being the owner or owners of any such property, shall knowingly use
or employ, or consent to the use or employment of the same as aforesaid, all such property is hereby declared to be lawful subject of prize
and capture wherever found; and it shall be the duty of the President
of the United States to cause the same to be seized, confiscated, and
condemned.

SEC. 2. *And be it further enacted,* That such prizes and capture shall be
condemned in the district or circuit court of the United States having
jurisdiction of the amount, or in admiralty in any district in which the

same may be seized, or into which they may be taken and proceedings first instituted.

SEC. 3. *And be it further enacted,* That the Attorney-General, or any district attorney of the United States in which said property may at the time be, may institute the proceedings of condemnation, and in such case they shall be wholly for the benefit of the United States; or any person may file an information with such attorney, in which case the proceedings shall be for the use of such informer and the United States in equal parts.

SEC. 4. *And be it further enacted,* That whenever hereafter, during the present insurrection against the Government of the United States, any person claimed to be held to labor or service under the law of any State, shall be required or permitted by the person to whom such labor or service is claimed to be due, or by the lawful agent of such person, to take up arms against the United States, or shall be required or permitted by the person to whom such labor or service is claimed to be due, or his lawful agent, to work or to be employed in or upon any fort, navy yard, dock, armory, ship, entrenchment, or in any military or naval service whatsoever, against the Government and lawful authority of the United States, then, and in every such case, the person to whom such labor or service is claimed to be due shall forfeit his claim to such labor, any law of the State or of the United States to the contrary notwithstanding. And whenever thereafter the person claiming such labor or service shall seek to enforce his claim, it shall be a full and sufficient answer to such claim that the person whose service or labor is claimed had been employed in hostile service against the Government of the United States, contrary to the provisions of this act.

Source

U.S. Statutes at Large, vol. 12, 319.

Appendix B

Browning–Lincoln Correspondence, September 1861

Quincy, Ills. Sept 17, 1861

Mr President

It is in no spirit of fault finding that I say I greatly regret the order modifying Genl Fremonts' proclamation.

That proclamation had the unqualified approval of every true friend of the Government within my knowledge. I do not know of an exception. Rebels and traitors, and all who sympathize with rebellion and treason, and who wish to see the government overthrown, would, of course, denounce it. Its influence was most salutary, and it was accomplishing much good. Its revocation disheartens our friends, and represses their ardor

It is true there is no express, written law authorizing it; but war is never carried on, and can never be, in strict accordance with previously adjusted constitutional and legal provisions. Have traitors who are warring upon the constitution and laws, and rejecting all their restraints, any right to invoke their protection?

Are they to be at liberty to use every weapon to accomplish the overthrow of the government, and are our hands to be so tied as to prevent the infliction of any injury upon them, or the successful resistance of their assaults?

The proclamation also provided that "All persons who shall be taken with arms in their hands within the lines shall be tried by court martial, and if found guilty, shall be shot."

I think there is no express statute law authorizing this, and yet, I believe, no body doubts its legality or propriety.

It does not conform to the act of Congress passed the 6th of August last, nor was it intended to; and yet it is neither revoked or modified by the order of Sept: 11th.

Is a traitors negro more sacred than his life? and is it true that the power which may dispose absolutely of the latter, is impotent to touch the former?

I am very sorry the order was made. It has produced a great deal of excitement, and is really filling the hearts of our friends with despondency.

It is rumored that Fremont is to be superceded. I hope this is not so. Coming upon the heels of the disapproval of his proclamation it would be a most unfortunate step, and would actually demoralize our cause throughout the North West. He has a very firm hold upon the confidence of the people.

You may rely upon what I say to you. You know that I am not in the habit of becoming needlessly excited, and that I have no ends to subserve except such as will advance the good of the country, and promote your own welfare—your fortune, and your fame.

I do think measures are sometimes shaped too much with a view to satisfy men of doubtful loyalty, instead of the true friends of the Country.

There has been too much tenderness towards traitors and rebels.

We must strike them terrible blows, and strike them hard and quick, or the government will go hopelessly to pieces.

As ever truly and faithfully
Your friend
O. H. Browning

Washington, Sep. 22. 1861
My dear Sir:

Yours of the 17th is just received; and, coming from you, I confess it astonishes me. That you should object to my adhering to a law which you had assisted in making, and presenting to me less than a month before, is odd enough—But this is a very small part—Genl

Fremont's proclamation, as to confiscation of property, and the liberation of slaves, is *purely political,* and not within the range of *military* law, or necessity. If a commanding General finds a necessity to seize the farm of a private owner, for a pasture, an encampment, or a fortification, he has the right to do so, and to so hold it, as long as the necessity lasts; and this is within military law, because within military necessity—But to say the farm shall no longer belong to the owner, or his heirs forever; and this as well when the farm is *not* needed for military purposes, as when it is, is purely political, without the savor of military law about it—And the same is true of slaves—If the General needs them, he can seize them and use them; but when the need is past, it is not for him to fix their permanent future condition—That must be settled according to laws made by law-makers, and not by military proclamations—The proclamation, in the point in question, is simply "dictatorship"—It assumes that the General may do *anything* he pleases—confiscate the lands and free the slaves of *loyal* people, as well as of disloyal ones—And going the whole figure I have no doubt would be more popular with some thoughtless people, than what has been done! But I can not assume the reckless position; nor allow others to assume it on my responsibility. You speak of it as being the only means of *saving* the government—On the contrary, it is itself the surrender of the government—Can it be pretended that it is any longer the government of the U. S.—any government of constitution & laws,—wherein a General, or a President may make permanent rules of property by proclamation—

I do not say Congress might not with propriety, pass a law, on the point, just such as Genl. Fremont proclaimed—I do not say I might not, as a member of Congress, vote for it—What I object to, is that I, as President, shall expressly, or impliedly, seize and exercise the permanent legislative functions of the government—

So much as to principle—Now as to policy—No doubt the thing was popular in some quarters, and would have been more so, if it had been a general declaration of emancipation—The Kentucky Legislature would not budge till that proclamation was modified; and Gen. Anderson telegraphed me, that on the news of Gen. Fremont having actually issued deeds of manumission, a whole company of our volunteers, threw down their arms and disbanded—I was so assured, as to think it probable, that the very arms we had furnished Kentucky, would be turned against us—I think to lose Kentucky, is nearly the

same as to lose the whole game—Kentucky gone, we can not hold
Missouri, nor as I think, Maryland—

These all against us, and the job on our hands is too large for
us—We would as well consent to separation at once, including
the surrender of the capital. On the contrary, if you will give up
your restlessness for new positions, and back me manfully on the
grounds upon which you & other kind friends gave me the election,
and have approved in my public documents, we shall go through
triumphantly—

You must not understand I took my course on the proclamation,
because of Kentucky—I took the same ground, in a private letter to the
General Fremont before I heard from Kentucky—

You think I am inconsistent because I did not also forbid Gen.
Fremont to shoot men under the proclamation—

I understand that part to be within military law; but I also think,
and so privately wrote Gen. Fremont, that it is impolitic in this,
that our adversaries have the power, and will certainly exercise it, to
shoot as many of our men as we shoot of theirs—I did not say this in
the public letter, because it is a subject I prefer not to discuss in the
hearing of our enemies—

There has been no thought of removing Gen. Fremont on any
ground connected with his proclamation; and if there has been any
wish for his removal on any ground, our mutual friend, Sam. Glover
can probably tell you what it was—I hope no real necessity for it exists
on any ground—

. . . .

Your friend as ever, A. Lincoln

Quincy, Illinois Sept 30, 1861
Mr President

Yours of the 22nd instant is before me. Aware of the multitude
and magnitude of your engagements, I certainly did not expect a
moment of your valuable time to be consumed in replying to any
communication of mine; but am, therefore, not the less obliged to you
for your very interesting letter.

Occasionally, since the beginning of our troubles, I have taken the liberty of writing you, and giving my opinions, valueless as they may be, upon the great questions which agitate the Nation, and which we are bound, however difficult and distressing they may be, in some way or other to solve.

I have also, from time to time, endeavored to give you a true reflection of public sentiment, so far as it was known to me. I have been prompted to this course by a very sincere, and unaffected interest in your individual welfare, fame, and fortune, as well as by a painfully intense anxiety for the maintainance of the Constitution and the Union; the restoration of the just authority of the government, and the triumph of as holy a cause, in my judgment, as ever engaged men's feelings and enlisted their energies.

I thought that whether the public sentiment here, and my own opinions, accorded with yours or not, you might still be not only willing, but glad to know them. I have, therefore, written to you frankly and candidly, but have, at all times, intended to be both kind and respectful; and regret it deeply if I have failed in either, as some passages in yours lead me to suspect I have. Indeed I fear I have only annoyed you. Nothing, I assure you, has been further from my purpose.

Fully appreciating the difficulties, and embarrassments of your position, I would be as ready and willing to aid and relieve you by any personal sacrifice I could make, as I would be reluctant to add to your labors and harrassments, either by fault finding or solicitations.

I have said many things to you which I have not said to others. Conscious of the great injury our cause would sustain by any weakening of the Confidence of the people in the administration, I have constantly vindicated both its men, and its measures, before the public; and when I have had complaints or suggestions to make, in regard to either, I have made them directly to you.

This, I thought, was demanded alike by the claims of friendship, and of patriotism

I am the partizan of no man. I would not sustain the nearest friend I have on earth in official misconduct, and would accord full praise to my bitterest foe in doing his duty to the Country.

In the conclusion of yours you say "Suppose you write to Hurlbut, and get him to resign."

I could not tell, for the life of me, whether you were serious, or whether you was Poking a little irony at me. If I thought you were in earnest I would certainly do it, as I could with great propriety, having in my possession his written pledge to resign if he drank a drop of liquor after going into the service. He has violated his pledge and behaved badly, and ought to resign.

What I said in regard to Genl. Fremont and his proclamation was in accordance with this feeling. My acquaintance with him is very limited and I have had no personal feeling in the matter.

If he was honestly and faithfully doing his duty, justice to him, and regards for the Country alike required that he should be sustained. There was much complaint and clamor against him, and, as I am not quick to take up evil report, I went twice to St Louis to see, and learn for myself all that I could. It is very probable he has made some mistakes. Most of us do; and he would be more than human if he were altogether exempt from the frailties of our nature: but, in the main, he seemed to be taking his measures wisely and well. Many of the charges against him appeared to me frivolous, and I did not know of any one who could take his position, and do better amid the surrounding difficulties; and was confident that his removal at the time, and under the circumstances, would be very damaging both to the administration, and the cause.

Hence I wrote you as I thought it my duty to do, certainly not intending any impertinent interference with executive affairs, or expecting what I said to have any greater scope than friendly suggestion.

This proclamation, in my opinion, embodies a true, and important principle which the government cannot afford to abandon, and with your permission, and with all deference to your opinions, so clearly expressed, I will venture, hastily to suggest my own views of the legal principles involved; for it is important that the law which governs the case should be certainly and clearly understood; and if you are right I am in very great error, which I ought to correct.

With your construction of the proclamation your reasoning is just, logical and conclusive, but either you have greatly misunderstood it, or I have.

According to my understanding of it, it does not touch the relations between the government and its citizens. It does not undertake to settle the rules of property between citizen and citizen. It does not deal with citizens at all, but with public enemies. It does not usurp a legislative function, but only declares a pre-existing law, and announces consequences which that law had already attached to given acts, and which would ensue as well without the proclamation as with it. It was, in fact, only a declaration of intention to live up to the international law settled centuries ago, and which was as much the law without the proclamation as with it. It was neither based upon the act of Congress of Augt. 6 1861, nor in collision with it, but had reference to a totally different class of cases, provided for long ago, by the political law of Nations.

The law of the 6th August acts upon and confiscates property because of the uses to which it is applied, wholly irrespective of the question of the loyalty or dis-loyalty of the owner. The property of a loyal citizen is as effectually forfeited if applied to the forbidden uses, as the property of a rebel, and the property of the traitor, in arms against the government, if not so applied, is as secure under the provisions of the statute as the property of the most loyal and devoted citizen. Rebels and loyalists stand on the same plat-form before the statute, and have an equality of right in no way affected by their friendship or hostility to the government.

Now, how is it with the proclamation?

As before remarked it is not based upon the statute, and has no reference whatever to the class of cases provided for by the Statute. It rests upon the well ascertained, and universally acknowledged principles of international political law as its foundation—upon the laws of war as acknowledged by all civilized Nations, and is in exact harmony with them.

The Confederate States, and all who acknowledge allegiance to the Confederate States, or take part with them, are public enemies. They are at war with the United States. Men taken in battle are held as prisoners; flags of truce pass between the hostile lines; intercourse is forbidden between certain States and parts of States; and sea-ports are formally blockaded.

These things constitute war, and all the rules of war apply, and all belligerent rights attack.

What are these rules and rights?

Burlamaqui says "By a state of war, that of society is abolished; so that whoever declares himself my enemy, gives me liberty to use violence against him in infinitum, or so far as I please &c."

The rebel States, by making war upon the United States, have dissolved the state of society which previously existed between them, and are no longer entitled to invoke the protection of the Constitution and laws which they have repudiated, and are endeavoring to destroy. All their property, both real and personal, is subject, by the law of nations, to be taken, and confiscated, and disposed of absolutely and forever by the belligerent power, without any reference whatever to the laws of society; and that as well without a proclamation to that effect as with it. A proclamation is but declaratory of the pre-existing law, and gives no additional force or effect to the law.

The same author continues

"The state of war, into which the enemy has put himself, and which it was in his own power to prevent, permits of itself every method that can be used against him; so that he has no reason to complain whatever we do."

"As to the goods of the enemy, it is certain that the state of war permits us to carry them off, to ravage, to spoil, or even entirely to destroy them; for as Cicero very well observes—It is not contrary to the law of nation nature to plunder a person whom we may lawfully kill."

"This right of spoil, or plunder extends in general to all things belonging to the enemy; and the law of Nations, properly so called, does not exempt even sacred things."

"In general it certainly is not lawful to plunder for plunder's sake, but it is just and innocent only, when it bears some relation to the design of the war; that is when an advantage directly accrues from it to ourselves, by appropriating these goods, or at least, when by ravaging and destroying them, we in some measure weaken the enemy."

Is there any question that the proclamation, carried into practical effect, would tend to our advantage by greatly weakening the enemy and diminishing his ability to carry on the war, and do us injury? This enquiry, however, belongs to the expediency of the measure, which I do not propose at present to discuss, but to confine myself to the question of rightful power and authority to adopt it.

The rules of law above stated declare the rights which war gives us over the effects of the enemy in a solemn war, declared in form between two states always distinct. Do the same principles apply to, and govern a civil war?

If so then the proclamation was not an excess of authority; was not in contravention of law; was not an invasion of any right of those to whom it related, and upon whom it acted, of which they could rightfully complain.

I believe civil wars are governed by the same rules which apply to and control what are technically called solemn wars, and that these rules embrace all who take part in the war against the government, whether the state where the hostile act is committed has formally thrown off the authority of the general government or not.

I quote again from Burlamaqui. "Grotius," says he, "pretends, that the right by which we acquire things taken in war, is so proper and peculiar to a solemn war, declared in form, that it has no force in others, as in civil wars &c., and that in the latter, in particular, there is no change of property, but in virtue of the sentence of a Judge.

We may observe, however, upon this point, that in most civil wars no common judge is acknowledged. If the state is monarchical, the dispute turns either upon the succession to the crown, or upon a considerable part of the states' pretending that the king has abused his power, in a manner which authorized his subjects to take up arms against him

In the former case, the very nature of the cause for which the war is undertaken, occasions the two parties of the state to form, as it were, two distinct bodies, till they come to agree upon a chief by some treaty. Hence, with respect to the two parties which were at war, it is on such treaty that the right depends, which persons may have to that which was taken on either side; and nothing hinders, but this right may be left on the same footing, and admitted to take place in the same manner, as in public wars between two states always distinct.

The other case, I mean an insurrection of a considerable part of the state against the reigning prince, can rarely happen, except when that prince has given room for it, either by tyranny, or by the violation of the fundamental laws of the kingdom.

Thus, the government is then dissolved, and the state is actually divided into two distinct and independent bodies; so that we are to form here the same judgment as in the former case.

For much stronger reasons does this take place in the Civil wars of a Republican state; in which the war, immediately of itself, destroys the sovereignty, which subsists solely in the union of its members."

It thus appears that when a state is actually divided into two distinct, and independent bodies, warring upon each other, they have no more right, as between each other, to claim the protection of the

Constitution and laws of the former government, than the citizens of a foreign state, at war with us would have a right to claim such protection.

The laws of civil society, that is, municipal laws and constitutions, as regulating intercourse between the parties, and determining their mutual and relative rights are dissolved, and the only rights which can be insisted upon are belligerent rights; and one of these is the right to take, confiscate and appropriate, or dispose of as we please, absolutely and forever, all the property, of every kind and character belonging to the enemy collectively and individually.

Now, the proclamation only declares, and, I think truly, the law as to one of our belligerent rights—"The property, real and personal, of all persons in the State of Missouri, who shall take up arms against the United States, or who shall be directly proven to have taken active part with their enemies in the field, is declared to be confiscated to the public use, and their slaves, if any they have, are hereby declared freemen."

It deals with public enemies only. It is, in terms, limited to those who are warring upon the government; and as to them it, in no sense, and to no extent, modifies the pre-existing law. It does not touch the loyal citizen or his rights of person or property, or at all intermeddle with the relations between him and his government or fix, or attempt to fix rules of property between the citizen and his government or between citizen and citizen. It is as limited in the class of persons upon whom it was to operate to public enemies, and was further territorially limited to the State of Missouri, and had no more application to or operation in Kentucky than in Australia.

I do not think it was an act of usurpation. I do not think it has in it any of the elements of dictatorship. I do think it was fully warranted by the laws of war, and in entire harmony with all the principles of international political law. I do further think that it is a high, important, and very valuable power which the government ought not to surrender, and without the exercise of which this war can never be brought to a successful termination. I do not speak this in reference to slaves alone, but to all property. Can the war be prosecuted upon the understanding that all the property captured from the enemy is to be held for restoration to former owners when the war is over?

If a general, in the progress of the war needs the horses of a loyal citizen for public use he may take them, but must make compensation for them, or restore them when the necessity has passed, making compensation for their use. But if he captures horses from those in arms against the government—from public enemies—are they not at his absolute disposal? May he not destroy them, sell them, or turn them loose upon the desert, according to the exigencies of the case, without accountability to any body? And if he may turn loose horses why may he not negroes? They both stand to us in the relation of property of the enemy, which we may lawfully take either to weaken him, or to strengthen ourselves. And if we have no right or power to take the negro, neither have we right or power to touch or take any other description of property belonging to our enemies. The consequence will be that while they act upon the laws of war and plunder us, and confiscate all our property, and cripple and weaken us, our hands are so tied as to disable us from touching any thing that is theirs.

If the proclamation had been limited to a confiscation of the horses and cattle of those in arms against the government and making war upon it for its overthrow, would the people of Kentucky, or any other State have objected, or would anyone have supposed there was an excess, or an abuse of power? And yet there is precisely the same right to extend it to negroes that there is to apply it to horses and cattle.

I think so valuable, so indispensable and vital a belligerent right ought not to be surrendered except upon the maturest consideration, and for the most cogent reasons.

The expediency of exercising the power is another question, and one about which men may well differ, and upon that I do not now propose to express any opinion. I did think, at the time, that it was expedient—that its influence was salutary, and that its fruit would be good, and nothing has fallen under my own observation to change that opinion.

But those who have a right to decide as well as think, have determined otherwise, and it becomes me, as well as every other good citizen, not only to submit to, but sustain that decision; and so I have done, and so I will continue to do.

This communication has grown to proportions far beyond my intentions when I commenced it, but even now it is only a glance at the important question discussed.

And now, Mr President, permit me in conclusion, in all kindness, to say that I am not conscious of any "restlessness for new positions." For us, new positions are not necessary. A firm adherence to old ones is, and this, I am sure, you intend. Thus far I have tried "to back you manfully upon the grounds upon which you had your election." It may be I have done it feebly, but certainly honestly and earnestly; and I will be one of the last to falter in support of either our principles, or their chosen exponent.

And I am very sure that neither for yourself, nor for the Country, do you more ardently desire "that we shall go through triumphantly," than does your very sincere

And faithful friend
O. H. Browning

Source

Text adapted from the Abraham Lincoln Papers at the Library of Congress, Manuscript Division (Washington, D.C.: American Memory Project, [2000–2002]), on the library's Internet site at http://memory.loc.gov/ammem/alhtml/alhome.html, transcribed by the Lincoln Studies Center, Knox College, Galesburg, Illinois.

Appendix C

Second Confiscation Act, July 17, 1862

CHAP. CXCV.—*An Act to suppress Insurrection, to punish Treason and Rebellion, to seize and confiscate the Property of Rebels, and for other Purposes.*

Be it enacted by the Senate and House of Representatives of the United States of America in Congress assembled, That every person who shall hereafter commit the crime of treason against the United States, and shall be adjudged guilty thereof, shall suffer death, and all his slaves, if any, shall be declared and made free; or, at the discretion of the court, he shall be imprisoned for not less than five years and fined not less than ten thousand dollars, and all his slaves, if any, shall be declared and made free; said fine shall be levied and collected on any or all of the property, real and personal, excluding slaves, of which the said person so convicted was the owner at the time of committing the said crime, any sale or conveyance to the contrary notwithstanding.

SEC. 2. *And be it further enacted,* That if any person shall hereafter incite, set on foot, assist, or engage in any rebellion or insurrection against the authority of the United States, or the laws thereof, or shall give aid or comfort thereto, or shall engage in, or give aid and comfort to, any such existing rebellion or insurrection, and be convicted thereof, such person shall be punished by imprisonment for a period not exceeding ten years, or by a fine not exceeding ten thousand dollars, and by the liberation of all his slaves, if any he have; or by both of said punishments, at the discretion of the court.

SEC. 3. *And be it further enacted,* That every person guilty of either of the offences described in this act shall be forever incapable and disqualified to hold any office under the United States.

SEC. 4. *And be it further enacted,* That this act shall not be construed in any way to affect or alter the prosecution, conviction, or punishment of any person or persons guilty of treason against the United States before the passage of this act, unless such person is convicted under this act.

SEC. 5. *And be it further enacted,* That, to insure the speedy termination of the present rebellion, it shall be the duty of the President of the United States to cause the seizure of all the estate and property, money, stocks, credits, and effects of the persons hereinafter named in this section, and to apply and use the same and the proceeds thereof for the support of the army of the United States, that is to say:

First. Of any person hereafter acting as an officer of the army or navy of the rebels in arms against the government of the United States.

Secondly. Of any person hereafter acting as President, Vice-President, member of Congress, judge of any court, cabinet officer, foreign minister, commissioner or consul of the so-called confederate states of America.

Thirdly. Of any person acting as governor of a state, member of a convention or legislature, or judge of any court of any of the so-called confederate states of America.

Fourthly. Of any person who, having held an office of honor, trust, or profit in the United States, shall hereafter hold an office in the so-called confederate states of America.

Fifthly. Of any person hereafter holding any office or agency under the government of the so-called confederate states of America, or under any of the several states of the said confederacy, or the laws thereof, whether such office or agency be national, state, or municipal in its name or character: *Provided,* That the persons, thirdly, fourthly, and fifthly above described shall have accepted their appointment or election since the date of the pretended ordinance of secession of the state, or shall have taken an oath of allegiance to, or to support the constitution of the so-called confederate states.

Sixthly. Of any person who, owning property in any loyal State or Territory of the United States, or in the District of Columbia, shall hereafter assist and give aid and comfort to such rebellion; and all sales, transfers, or conveyances of any such property shall be null and void; and it shall be a sufficient bar to any suit brought by such person for the possession or the use of such property, or any of it, to allege and prove that he is one of the persons described in this section.

SEC. 6. *And be it further enacted,* That if any person within any State or Territory of the United States, other than those named as aforesaid, after the passage of this act, being engaged in armed rebellion against the government of the United States, or aiding or abetting such rebellion shall not, within sixty days after public warning and proclamation duly given and made by the President of the United States, cease to aid, countenance, and abet such rebellion, and return to his allegiance to the United States, all the estate and property, moneys, stocks, and credits of such person shall be liable to seizure as aforesaid, and it shall be the duty of the President to seize and use them as aforesaid or the proceeds thereof And all sales, transfers, or conveyances, of any such property after the expiration of the said sixty days from the date of such warning and proclamation shall be null and void; and it shall be a sufficient bar to any suit brought by such person for the possession or the use of such property, or any of it, to allege and prove that he is one of the persons described in this section.

SEC. 7. *And be it further enacted,* That to secure the condemnation and sale of any of such property, after the same shall have been seized, so that it may be made available for the purpose aforesaid, proceedings in rem shall be instituted in the name of the United States in any district court thereof, or in any territorial court, or in the United States district court for the District of Columbia, within which the property above described, or any part thereof, may be found, or into which the same, if movable, may first be brought, which proceedings shall conform as nearly as may be to proceedings in admiralty or revenue cases, and if said property, whether real or personal, shall be found to have belonged to a person engaged in rebellion, or who has given aid or comfort thereto, the same shall be condemned as enemies' property and become the property of the United States, and may be disposed of as the court shall decree and the proceeds thereof paid into the treasury of the United States for the purposes aforesaid.

SEC. 8. *And be it further enacted,* That the several courts aforesaid shall have power to make such orders, establish such forms of decree and sale, and direct such deeds and conveyances to be executed and delivered by the marshals thereof where real estate shall be the subject of sale, as shall fitly and efficiently effect the purposes of this act, and vest in the purchasers of such property good and valid titles thereto. And the said courts shall have power to allow such fees and charges of their officers as shall be reasonable and proper in the premises.

SEC. 9. *And be it further enacted,* That all slaves of persons who shall hereafter be engaged in rebellion against the government of the United States, or who shall in any way give aid or comfort thereto, escaping from such persons and taking refuge within the lines of the army; and all slaves captured from such persons or deserted by them and coming under the control of the government of the United States; and all slaves of such persons found on [*sic*] being within any place occupied by rebel forces and afterwards occupied by the forces of the United States, shall be deemed captives of war, and shall be forever free of their servitude, and not again held as slaves.

SEC. 10. *And be it further enacted,* That no slave escaping into any State, Territory, or the District of Columbia, from any other State, shall be delivered up, or in any way impeded or hindered of his liberty, except for crime, or some offence against the laws, unless the person claiming said fugitive shall first make oath that the person to whom the labor or service of such fugitive is alleged to be due is his lawful owner, and has not borne arms against the United States in the present rebellion, nor in any way given aid and comfort thereto; and no person engaged in the military or naval service of the United States shall, under any pretence whatever, assume to decide on the validity of the claim of any person to the service or labor of any other person, or surrender up any such person to the claimant, on pain of being dismissed from the service.

SEC. 11. *And be it further enacted,* That the President of the United States is authorized to employ as many persons of African descent as he may deem necessary and proper for the suppression of this rebellion, and for this purpose he may organize and use them in such manner as he may judge best for the public welfare.

SEC. 12. *And be it further enacted,* That the President of the United States is hereby authorized to make provision for the transportation, colonization, and settlement, in some tropical country beyond the limits of the United States, of such persons of the African race, made free by the provisions of this act, as may be willing to emigrate, having first obtained the consent of the government of said country to their protection and settlement within the same, with all the rights and privileges of freemen.

SEC. 13. *And be it further enacted,* That the President is hereby authorized, at any time hereafter, by proclamation, to extend to persons who may have participated in the existing rebellion in any State or part thereof, pardon and amnesty, with such exceptions and at such time and on such conditions as he may deem expedient for the public welfare.

SEC. 14. *And be it further enacted,* That the courts of the United States shall have full power to institute proceedings, make orders and decrees, issue process, and do all other things necessary to carry this act into effect.

Source

U.S. Statutes at Large, vol. 12, 589–92.

Appendix D

Emancipation Proclamation, First Draft, July 22, 1862

In pursuance of the sixth section of the act of congress entitled "An act to suppress insurrection and to punish treason and rebellion, to seize and confiscate property of rebels, and for other purposes" Approved July 17, 1862, and which act, and the Joint Resolution explanatory thereof, are herewith published, I, Abraham Lincoln, President of the United States, do hereby proclaim to, and warn all persons within the contemplation of said sixth section to cease participating in, aiding, countenancing, or abetting the existing rebellion, or any rebellion against the government of the United States, and to return to their proper allegiance to the United States, on pain of the forfeitures and seizures, as within and by said sixth section provided—

And I hereby make known that it is my purpose, upon the next meeting of Congress, to again recommend the adoption of a practical measure for tendering pecuniary aid to the free choice or rejection, of any and all States which may then be recognizing and practically sustaining the authority of the United States, and which may then have voluntarily adopted, or thereafter may voluntarily adopt, gradual abolishment of slavery within such State or States—that the object is to practically restore, thenceforward to be maintain[ed], the constitutional relation between the general government, and each, and all the states, wherein that relation is now suspended, or disturbed; and that, for this object, the war, as it has been, will be, prosecuted. And, as a fit and necessary military measure for effecting this object, I, as Commander-in-Chief of the Army and Navy of the United States, do order and declare that on the first day of January in the year of our Lord one thousand, eight hundred and sixty three, all persons held as slaves within any state or states, wherein the constitutional authority of the United States shall not then be practically recognized, submitted to, and maintained, shall then, thenceforward, and forever, be free.

Source

Collected Works of Abraham Lincoln, vol. 5, 336–37 (R. P. Basler ed. 1953).

Appendix E

Preliminary Emancipation Proclamation, September 22, 1862

By the President of the United States of America
A Proclamation.

I, Abraham Lincoln, President of the United States of America, and Commander-in-chief of the Army and Navy thereof, do hereby proclaim and declare that hereafter, as heretofore, the war will be prosecuted for the object of practically restoring the constitutional relation between the United States, and each of the states, and the people thereof, in which states that relation is, or may be suspended, or disturbed.

That it is my purpose, upon the next meeting of Congress to again recommend the adoption of a practical measure tendering pecuniary aid to the free acceptance or rejection of all slave-states, so called, the people whereof may not then be in rebellion against the United States, and which states, may then have voluntarily adopted, or thereafter may voluntarily adopt, immediate, or gradual abolishment of slavery within their respective limits; and that the effort to colonize persons of African descent, with their consent, upon this continent, or elsewhere, with the previously obtained consent of the Governments existing there, will be continued.

That on the first day of January in the year of our Lord, one thousand eight hundred and sixty-three, all persons held as slaves within any state, or designated part of a state, the people whereof shall then be in rebellion against the United States shall be then, thenceforward, and forever free; and the executive government of the United States, including the military and naval authority thereof, will recognize and maintain the freedom of such persons, and will do no act or acts to repress such persons, or any of them, in any efforts they may make for their actual freedom.

That the executive will, on the first day of January aforesaid, by proclamation, designate the States, and parts of states, if any, in which the people thereof respectively, shall then be in rebellion against the United States; and the fact that any state, or the people thereof shall, on that day be, in good faith represented in the Congress of the United States, by members chosen thereto, at elections wherein a majority of the qualified voters of such state shall have participated, shall, in the absence of strong countervailing testimony, be deemed conclusive evidence that such state and the people thereof, are not then in rebellion against the United States.

That attention is hereby called to an act of Congress entitled "An act to make an additional Article of War" approved March 13, 1862, and which act is in the words and figure following:

Be it enacted by the Senate and House of Representatives of the United States of America in Congress assembled, That hereafter the following shall be promulgated as an additional article of war for the government of the army of the United States, and shall be obeyed and observed as such:

Article—. All officers or persons in the military or naval service of the United States are prohibited from employing any of the forces under their respective commands for the purpose of returning fugitives from service or labor, who may have escaped from any persons to whom such service or labor is claimed to be due, and any officer who shall be found guilty by a court-martial of violating this article shall be dismissed from the service.

SEC. 2. *And be it further enacted,* That this act shall take effect from and after its passage.

Also to the ninth and tenth sections of an act entitled "An Act to suppress Insurrection, to punish Treason and Rebellion, to seize and confiscate property of rebels, and for other purposes," approved July 17, 1862, and which sections are in the words and figures following:

SEC. 9. *And be it further enacted,* That all slaves of persons who shall hereafter be engaged in rebellion against the government of the United States, or who shall in any way give aid or comfort thereto, escaping from such persons and taking refuge within the lines of the army; and all slaves captured from such persons or deserted by them and coming under the control of the government of the United States; and all slaves of such persons found *on* (or) being within any place occupied by rebel forces and afterwards occupied by the forces of the United States, shall be deemed captives of war, and shall be forever free of their servitude and not again held as slaves.

SEC. 10. *And be it further enacted,* That no slave escaping into any State, Territory, or the District of Columbia, from any other State, shall be delivered up, or in any way impeded or hindered of his liberty, except for crime, or some offence against the laws, unless the person claiming said fugitive shall first make oath that the person to whom the labor or service of such fugitive is alleged to be due is his lawful owner, and has not borne arms against the United States in the present rebellion, nor in any way given aid and comfort thereto; and no person engaged in the military or naval service of the United States shall, under any pretence whatever, assume to decide on the validity of the claim of any person to the service or labor of any other person, or surrender up any such person to the claimant, on pain of being dismissed from the service.

And I do hereby enjoin upon and order all persons engaged in the military and naval service of the United States to observe, obey, and enforce, within their respective spheres of service, the act, and sections above recited.

And the executive will in due time recommend that all citizens of the United States who shall have remained loyal thereto throughout the rebellion, shall (upon the restoration of the constitutional relation between the United States, and their respective states, and people, if that relation shall have been suspended or disturbed) be compensated for all losses by acts of the United States, including the loss of slaves.

In witness whereof, I have hereunto set my hand, and caused the seal of the United States to be affixed.

Done at the City of Washington, this twenty second day of September, in the year of our Lord, one thousand eight hundred and sixty two, and of the Independence of the United States, the eighty seventh.

By the President: ABRAHAM LINCOLN

WILLIAM H. SEWARD, Secretary of State.

Source

Collected Works of Abraham Lincoln, vol. 5, 433–36 (R. P. Basler ed. 1953).

Final Emancipation Proclamation, January 1, 1863

By the President of the United States of America
A Proclamation

Whereas, on the twenty-second day of September, in the year of our Lord one thousand eight hundred and sixty-two, a proclamation was issued by the President of the United States, containing, among other things, the following, to wit:

> "That on the first day of January, in the year of our Lord one thousand eight hundred and sixty-three, all persons held as slaves within any State or designated part of a State, the people whereof shall then be in rebellion against the United States, shall be then, thenceforward, and forever free; and the Executive Government of the United States, including the military and naval authority thereof, will recognize and maintain the freedom of such persons, and will do no act or acts to repress such persons, or any of them, in any efforts they may make for their actual freedom.
>
> "That the Executive will, on the first day of January aforesaid, by proclamation, designate the States and parts of States, if any, in which the people thereof, respectively, shall then be in rebellion against the United States; and the fact that any State, or the people thereof, shall on that day be, in good faith, represented in the Congress of the United States by members

chosen thereto at elections wherein a majority of the qualified voters of such State shall have participated, shall, in the absence of strong countervailing testimony, be deemed conclusive evidence that such State, and the people thereof, are not then in rebellion against the United States."

Now, therefore I, Abraham Lincoln, President of the United States, by virtue of the power in me vested as Commander-in-Chief, of the Army and Navy of the United States in time of actual armed rebellion against the authority and government of the United States, and as a fit and necessary war measure for suppressing said rebellion, do, on this first day of January, in the year of our Lord one thousand eight hundred and sixty-three, and in accordance with my purpose so to do publicly proclaimed for the full period of one hundred days, from the day first above mentioned, order and designate as the States and parts of States wherein the people thereof respectively, are this day in rebellion against the United States, the following, to wit:

Arkansas, Texas, Louisiana, (except the Parishes of St. Bernard, Plaquemines, Jefferson, St. John, St. Charles, St. James Ascension, Assumption, Terrebonne, Lafourche, St. Mary, St. Martin, and Orleans, including the City of New Orleans) Mississippi, Alabama, Florida, Georgia, South Carolina, North Carolina, and Virginia, (except the forty-eight counties designated as West Virginia, and also the counties of Berkley, Accomac, Northampton, Elizabeth City, York, Princess Ann, and Norfolk, including the cities of Norfolk and Portsmouth); and which excepted parts, are for the present, left precisely as if this proclamation were not issued.

And by virtue of the power, and for the purpose aforesaid, I do order and declare that all persons held as slaves within said designated States, and parts of States, are, and henceforward shall be free; and that the Executive government of the United States, including the military and naval authorities thereof, will recognize and maintain the freedom of said persons.

And I hereby enjoin upon the people so declared to be free to abstain from all violence, unless in necessary self-defence; and I recommend to them that, in all cases when allowed, they labor faithfully for reasonable wages.

And I further declare and make known, that such persons of suitable condition, will be received into the armed service of the United States to garrison forts, positions, stations, and other places, and to man vessels of all sorts in said service.

And upon this act, sincerely believed to be an act of justice, warranted by the Constitution, upon military necessity, I invoke the considerate judgment of mankind, and the gracious favor of Almighty God.

In witness whereof, I have hereunto set my hand and caused the seal of the United States to be affixed.

Done at the City of Washington, this first day of January, in the year of our Lord one thousand eight hundred and sixty three, and of the Independence of the United States of America the eighty-seventh.

By the President: ABRAHAM LINCOLN

WILLIAM H. SEWARD, Secretary of State.

Source

Collected Works of Abraham Lincoln, vol. 6, 28–30 (R. P. Basler ed. 1953).

Notes

Introduction

1. *Collected Works of Abraham Lincoln* (hereafter cited as *Collected Works*), vol. 6, 406 (R. P. Basler ed. 1953).

1. Planting the Seed

1. D. H. Donald, *Charles Sumner and the Coming of the Civil War*, 388 (1961).

2. In reference to the blockade proclamation, Thaddeus Stevens claimed that Lincoln had said, "I don't know anything about the law of nations." *Recollected Words of Abraham Lincoln*, 423 (D. Fehrenbacher and V. Fehrenbacher eds. 1996). According to Assistant Attorney General Titian Coffey, Lincoln told Attorney General Edward Bates, "I am not much of a prize lawyer." *Reminiscences of Abraham Lincoln by Distinguished Men of His Time*, 245 (A. T. Rice ed. 1971 reprint of 1888 ed.). "Prize law" was a part of the law of war that dealt with the capture of enemy vessels at sea.

3. First Inaugural Address, March 4, 1861, *Collected Works*, vol. 4, 262.

4. "It was a generally accepted axiom of American constitutional law in 1861 that slavery was a domestic institution of the States, and that as a State institution it was outside Federal jurisdiction." James G. Randall, *Constitutional Problems under Lincoln*, 343 (rev. ed. 1951).

5. Browning to Lincoln, April 18, 1861, Abraham Lincoln Papers at the Library of Congress, Manuscript Division (Washington, D.C.: American Memory Project, [2000–2002]), on the Library's Internet site at http://memory.loc.gov/ammem/alhtml/alhome.html.

6. Browning to Lincoln, April 30, 1861, Abraham Lincoln Papers at the Library of Congress, http://memory.loc.gov/ammem/alhtml/alhome.html.

7. John K. Mahon, *The War of 1812*, 312–15 (1991 reprint).

8. John B. Moore, *History and Digest of International Arbitrations to Which the United States has been a Party*, vol. 1, 351 (1898).

9. Randall, *Constitutional Problems under Lincoln,* 344 (rev. ed. 1951).

10. Robert V. Remini, *John Quincy Adams,* 137–41 (2002).

11. William L. Miller, *Arguing about Slavery,* 206–9 (1996).

12. Quoted in William Whiting, *The War Powers of the President, and The Legislative Powers of Congress in Relation to Rebellion, Treason and Slavery,* 77 (4th ed. 1863).

13. Ibid., 78–79.

14. *Brown v. United States,* 12 U.S. (8 Cranch) 110, 145 (1814) (Story, J. dissenting); ibid. at 152.

15. Joseph Story, *Commentaries on the Constitution of the United States,* ch. XXI, sec. 1172 (1833).

16. J. L. Brierly, *The Law of Nations,* 1 (6th ed. 1963); ibid., 59.

17. Frederick W. Marks, *Independence on Trial,* 3–15 (1972).

18. See the case of *Respublica v. DeLongchamps,* 1 U.S. (1 Dallas) 111 (Philadelphia, Pa., Court of Oyer and Terminer, 1784).

19. John S. D. Eisenhower, *Agent of Destiny: The Life and Times of General Winfield Scott,* 148 (1997).

20. Ibid., 146–47; Kenneth W. Porter, *The Black Seminoles,* 40–43 (1996).

21. Eisenhower, *Agent of Destiny,* 149–67.

22. Quoted in Porter, *The Black Seminoles,* 78 (1996).

23. Ibid., 95.

24. K. Jack Bauer, *Zachary Taylor,* 86 (paperback ed. 1993); Whiting, *The War Powers of the President,* 76–77.

25. Miller, *Arguing about Slavery,* 444–54.

26. Quoted in Whiting, *The War Powers of the President,* 80.

27. Ibid.

28. "Decree for the Emancipation of Slaves," June 2, 1816, in *El Libertador: Writings of Simon Bolivar,* 177 (F. Fornoff trans. 2003). See also *Colombia, A Country Study* 19 (Federal Research Division, Library of Congress, 1990); John V. Lombardi, *Venezuela: The Search for Order, the Dream of Progress,* 148–50, 176 (1982); Gerhard Masur, *Simon Bolivar,* 192–98 (Venezuela, 1816), 275–76 (Columbia, 1819) (2nd ed. 1969).

29. Randall, *Constitutional Problems under Lincoln,* 375, footnote 6 (1951 reprint).

30. Fort Mose Historical Society Internet site, http://www.oldcity.com/mose/; accessed on February 22, 2000.

31. Darcie Macmahon and Kathleen Deagan, "Legacy of Fort Mose," *Archaeology* vol. 49, no. 5 (September–October 1996). The site of Fort Mose has been located and excavated by University of Florida archaeologists. In 1994, it was declared a national historic landmark as the first free black community in North America.

32. "Haiti—Toussaint Louverture," on the Library of Congress Internet

site at: http://lcweb2.loc.gov/frd/cs/httoc.html#ht0018; accessed February 22, 2000.

33. Sidney Kaplan and Emma Kaplan, *The Black Presence in the Era of the American Revolution,* 73 (footnote) (rev. ed. 1989).

34. Kirsten Schultz, *Tropical Versailles,* 173 (paperback ed. 2001).

35. Kaplan and Kaplan, *The Black Presence in the Era of the American Revolution,* 73–74; ibid., 76.

36. Ibid., 78; 79, figure 60; Charles Johnson and Patricia Smith, *Africans in America: America's Journey through Slavery,* 178 (1998).

37. Johnson and Smith, *Africans in America,* 195; ibid., 197.

38. K. Jack Bauer, *The Mexican War,* 223, 253, 326–35 (1974); Bauer, *Zachary Taylor,* 212–13 (1985); Eisenhower, *Agent of Destiny,* 52, 78 (1997).

39. *Luther v. Borden,* 48 U.S. (7 Howard) 1, 45–46 (1849) (emphasis added).

40. Remini, *John Quincy Adams,* 153–55 (2002).

41. Arthur Nussbaum, *A Concise History of the Law of Nations,* 162 (rev. ed. 1954).

42. Moore, *History and Digest of International Arbitrations,* vol. 1, 351.

43. 12 U.S. (8 Cranch) 109 (1814).

44. Randall, *Constitutional Problems under Lincoln,* 375, footnote 6 (1951 reprint).

2. The Supreme Court on Private Property and War

1. 12 U.S. (8 Cranch) 109 (1814).

2. Ibid. at 121.

3. An Act respecting Alien Enemies, July 6, 1798, 1 Stat. 577. This act is still in force, and in its current form appears in Title 50 of the U.S. Code, sections 21–22.

4. 54 U.S. 115 (1851).

5. Doniphan's campaign is described in Bauer, *The Mexican War,* 151–58 (1974).

6. 54 U.S. at 134.

7. General Order 1, Headquarters, Department of Missouri, January 1, 1862, in *War of the Rebellion: A Compilation of the Official Records of the Union and Confederate Armies* (hereafter *Official Records*), series 2, vol. 2, 247, 249.

8. Article 57, General Order 100, War Department, Adjutant General's Office, April 24, 1863, *Official Records,* series 2, vol. 5, 671.

9. "Treating, in the field, the rebellious enemy according to the law and usages of war has never prevented the legitimate government from trying the leaders of the rebellion or chief rebels for high treason, and from treating them accordingly, unless they are included in a general amnesty." Article 154, Gen-

eral Order 100, War Department, Adjutant General's Office, April 24, 1863, *Official Records,* series 2, vol. 5, 671.

10. See Stanton to Wool, February 26, 1862, *Official Records,* series 2, vol. 3, 22; Scott to Halleck, February 19, 1862, ibid., 280; Buell to Halleck, February 19, 1862, ibid., 283.

11. Meigs to Cameron, July 12, 1861, *Official Records,* series 2, vol. 3, 8.

12. For a description of the institutions of parole and exchange, see Gerald J. Prokopowicz, "Word of Honor: The Parole Systems in the Civil War," *North and South* vol. 6, no. 4, 24 (May 2003).

13. Ibid.

14. When British forces in South Carolina executed an American prisoner for parole violation during the American Revolution, the incident was regarded as extraordinary on both sides of the Atlantic. Larry G. Bowman, *Captured Americans,* 101–3 (1976). Napoleon, a ruler not noted for soft treatment of his opponents, ordered that enemy officers caught violating parole would be punished by being treated as enlisted prisoners. Imperial Decree of 4 August 1811 Concerning Prisoners of War and Hostages, in Howard S. Levie, *Documents on Prisoners of War,* 17 (1979, Naval War College International Law Studies vol. 60). In April 1862, Major Lee, the judge advocate of the U.S. Army, expressed doubts that death was appropriate for parole violators except in aggravated circumstances. *In the matter of Ebenezer Magoffin, Official Records,* series 2, vol. 1, 369–73.

15. George G. Lewis and John Mewha, *History of Prisoner of War Utilization by the United States Army 1776–1945,* 6 (1955, Department of the Army Pamphlet 20–213).

16. See "French National Convention Decree of May 25, 1793, on A Uniform Method for the Exchange of Prisoners," in Levie, *Documents on Prisoners of War,* 14 (1979).

17. First Article, "Cartel for the Exchange of Prisoners of War between Great Britain and the United States of America," May 12, 1813, in Levie, *Documents on Prisoners of War,* 18–19.

18. See Joshua Rozenberg, "Prosecution in Britain Would Face Difficulties," *Daily Telegraph,* July 7, 2003.

19. General Order 1, Headquarters, Department of Missouri, January 1, 1862, *Official Records,* series 2, vol. 2, 247, 249.

20. General Order 100, War Department, Adjutant General's Office, April 24, 1863, *Official Records,* series 2, vol. 5, 671.

21. Case of John W. Owen, *Official Records,* series 2, vol. 1, 406–27.

22. Ibid., 407.

23. Trial of Colonel Ebenezer Magoffin, February 6–20, 1862, *Official Records,* series 2, vol. 1, 292 et seq.

24. *Official Records,* series 2, vol. 1, 255–56.

25. Ibid., 258–59.

26. See Douglas Jehl and Michael Gordon, "American Forces Reach Cease-Fire with Terror Group," *New York Times*, April 29, 2003.

27. At a cabinet meeting on December 10, 1861, for example, Attorney General Bates opposed the negotiation of a general cartel for the exchange of prisoners of war, believing this would accord further recognition to the Confederacy. *Inside Lincoln's Cabinet: The Civil War Diaries of Salmon P. Chase*, 49 (D. Donald ed. 1954).

28. Telegram from Secretary of War Stanton to Lieutenant General Ulysses S. Grant, March 3, 1865, *Collected Works*, vol. 8, 330–31.

29. William K. Klingamen, *Abraham Lincoln and the Road to Emancipation*, 52, 65 (2001).

30. Quoted in Harry Jaffa, *A New Birth of Freedom*, 215 (2000).

31. "Act to make an additional Article of War," March 13, 1862, 12 Stat. 354. On July 9, 1861, the House of Representatives had adopted a resolution that "in the judgment of this House it is no part of the duty of the soldiers of the United States to capture and return fugitives." *Official Records*, series 2, vol. 1, 759. In December, Congressman Owen Lovejoy, an Illinois abolitionist, introduced legislation to turn this nonbinding resolution into law by amending the Articles of War. Allen C. Guelzo, *Lincoln's Emancipation Proclamation*, 64 (2004).

32. Lincoln to George Robertson, November 26, 1862, *Collected Works*, vol. 5, 512.

33. See Lowell H. Harrison, *Lincoln of Kentucky*, 233–35 (2000).

3. Criminal Conspiracy or War?

1. Farewell Address at Springfield, Illinois, February 11, 1861, *Collected Works*, vol. 4, 190–91.

2. Special Message to Congress, July 4, 1861, *Collected Works*, vol. 4, 421, 438–39.

3. Harold Holzer, *Washington and Lincoln Portrayed: National Icons in Popular Prints*, 173 (1993).

4. Kevin T. Barksdale, "Our Rebellious Neighbors: Virginia Border Counties during Pennsylvania's Whiskey Rebellion," *Virginia Magazine of History and Biography*, vol. 111, 5, 10 (2003).

5. Proclamation of September 25, 1794, in *George Washington: A Collection*, 598–99 (W. B. Allen ed. 1988).

6. Proclamation of August 7, 1794, in ibid., 589, 590.

7. Proclamation of September 25, 1794, in ibid., 599.

8. J. Flexner, *George Washington: Anguish and Farewell (1793–1799)*, 177 (1969).

9. M. Holt, *The Rise and Fall of the American Whig Party*, 20–23 (1999);

Eisenhower, *Agent of Destiny*, 133–40 (1997); M. Peterson, *The Great Triumvirate: Webster, Clay and Calhoun*, 212–31 (1987).

10. David H. Donald, *Lincoln*, 302–3 (1995).

11. For example, Thaddeus Stevens, in *Recollected Words of Abraham Lincoln*, 423 (Fehrenbacher and Fehrenbacher eds. 1996).

12. Brian R. Dirck, *Lincoln and Davis: Imagining America, 1809–1865* (2002).

13. Article 3, section 3.

14. Proclamation Calling Forth Militia and Convening Congress, April 15, 1861, *Collected Works*, vol. 4, 331–32.

15. Ibid. (emphasis added).

16. Isham G. Harris to Simon Cameron, April 17, 1861, *Official Records*, series 3, vol. 1, 81.

17. Isham G. Harris to Lincoln, April 29, 1861, Abraham Lincoln Papers at the Library of Congress, http://memory.loc.gov/ammem/alhtml/alhome. html.

18. Lincoln to Isham G. Harris, May [1?] 1861, *Collected Works*, vol. 4, 351. The president's suspicions of Governor Harris were justified. Tennessee seceded and joined the Confederacy under Harris's leadership, and Harris fled the state when Nashville was occupied by U.S. forces in early 1862. He was serving as an aide to Confederate general Albert Sidney Johnson when the latter was killed at the battle of Shiloh.

19. 54 U.S. at 134.

20. See Dean B. Mahin, *One War at a Time*, 50–52 (1999).

21. Title 18, U.S. Code, section 1651. The Supreme Court upheld the constitutionality of so defining piracy in *United States v. Smith*, 5 Wheaton 153 (1820).

22. David J. Eicher, *The Longest Night*, 54 (2001)

23. Scott S. Sheads and Daniel C. Toomey, *Baltimore during the Civil War*, 23, 35 (1997).

24. To the Commanding General of the Army of the United States, April 27, 1861, *Official Records*, series 2, vol. 2, 19, 20.

25. *Ex parte Merryman*, 17 Fed. Cas. 144 (Circuit Court, District of Maryland, 1861) (Case No. 9,487).

26. *Luther v. Borden*, 48 U.S. (7 Howard) 1, 45–46 (1849).

27. Special Message to Congress, July 4, 1861, *Collected Works*, vol. 4, 421.

28. See, for example, the case of *The Justices v. Murray*, 76 U.S. 658 (1870).

29. Edward Bates to the president, July 5, 1861, *Official Records*, series 2, vol. 2, 20 et seq.

30. Under English and American common law, the writ of replevin was a court order requiring a person who was wrongfully holding personal property of another to either return the property or pay the owner its value.

31. Winfield Scott to Lieutenant Colonel Martin Burke, August 2, 1861, *Official Records*, series 2, vol. 1, 636.

32. See Mark E. Neely, *The Fate of Liberty*, 137 (1991).

33. William Cranston to William H. Seward, August 26, 1861, *Official Records*, series 2, vol. 2, 48; Seward to Cranston, August 31, ibid., 49.

34. Seward to John S. Keyes, September 23, 1861, *Official Records*, series 2, vol. 2, 75.

35. Assistant Adjutant General E. D. Townsend to Colonel Henry L. Scott, August 26, 1861, and Henry L. Scott to Lieutenant Colonel Charles F. Smith, August 27, 1861, *Official Records*, series 2, vol. 2, 48.

36. Lincoln, Presidential Order, July 31, 1861, *Official Records*, series 2 vol. 2, 37.

37. Carr to Cameron, September 3, 1861; Cameron to Carr, September 3, 1861, *Official Records*, series 2, vol. 2, 54.

38. John A. Kennedy to Seward, September 14, 1861, *Official Records*, series 2, vol. 2, 496. The *Daily News*, an organ of New York's pro-Southern mayor Fernando Wood, voluntarily ceased publication on September 14, 1861, to protest restrictions on freedom of speech. Ibid.

39. Carr to Cameron, September 11, 1861, *Official Records*, series 2, vol. 2, 60.

40. Memoranda of Various Political Arrests, *Official Records*, series 2, vol. 2, 302.

41. Nathan Hubbell to Lincoln, September 21, 1861, *Official Records*, series 2, vol. 2, 73.

42. McClellan to Buell, November 12, 1861, *Official Records*, series 2, vol. 2, 136.

43. General Sherman to General Ward, November 27, 1861, *Official Records*, series 2, vol. 2, 125–26.

44. D. C. Buell to L. Thomas, December 5, 1861, *Official Records*, series 2, vol. 2, 170.

45. Edward S. Bates to the secretary of war, December 30, 1861, *Official Records*, series 2, vol. 2, 182.

4. The Union Applies the Law of War

1. Assistant Adjutant General Williams to Colonel Bowen, May 18, 1861, *Official Records*, series 2, vol. 3, 1; Assistant Adjutant General Fry to Mr. Johnson, June 27, 1861, *Official Records*, series 2, vol. 2, 12.

2. McClellan to Scott, June 28, 1861, *Official Records*, series 2, vol. 2, 14.

3. McClellan to Townsend, July 13, 1861, *Official Records*, series 2, vol. 3, 9.

4. Meigs to Cameron, July 12, 1861, *Official Records*, series 2, vol. 3, 8.

5. Special Order 284, War Department, Washington, October 23, 1861, *Official Records*, series 2, vol. 3, 121.

6. General Scott to General McClellan, July 14, 1861, *Official Records*, series 2, vol. 3, 9–11.

7. Governor Dennison to Secretary Cameron, August 7 and 14, 1864, *Official Records*, series 2, vol. 2, 39, 42.

8. General Scott to Lieutenant Colonel Burke, July 19, 1861, *Official Records*, series 2, vol. 2, 32.

9. General Scott to Dimick, October 19, 1861, *Official Records*, series 2, vol. 2, 110–11; Seward to Keyes, November 13, 1861, *Official Records*, series 2, vol. 2, 137.

10. Proclamation of a Blockade, April 19, 1861, *Collected Works*, vol. 4, 338–39.

11. Flag Officer Stringham to Secretary of the Navy Welles, June 6, 1861, *Official Records*, series 2, vol. 3, 1–2.

12. Davis to Lincoln, July 6, 1861, *Official Records*, series 2, vol. 3, 5–6.

13. Testimony of Charles W. Page, *United States v. William Smith*, October 22, 1861 (U.S. District Court for the Eastern District of Pa.), *Official Records*, series 2, vol. 3, 58, 69.

14. Colonel Cogswell to General Thomas, November 11, 1861, *Official Records*, series 2, vol. 3, 130–31.

15. General Wool to Adjutant General Thomas, January 24, 1862, *Official Records*, series 2, vol. 3, 212.

16. General Huger, C.S. Army, to General Wool, U.S. Army, January 27, 1862, *Official Records*, series 2, vol. 3, 217.

17. Seward to U.S. marshals, January 31, 1862, *Official Records*, series 2, vol. 3, 229; General Wool to General Huger, February 10, 1862, ibid., 250.

18. Seward to the president, August 2, 1861, *Official Records*, series 2, vol. 2, 37; General Dix to General Wool, August 22, 1861, ibid., vol. 3, 27–28.

19. *Inside Lincoln's Cabinet*, 49 (Donald ed. 1954).

20. General Grant to General Polk, October 14, 1861, *Official Records*, series 2, vol. 1, 511.

21. General Smith to General Pillow, November 26, 1861, *Official Records*, series 2, vol. 1, 523.

22. See, for example, Adjutant General Thomas to General Wool, November 29, 1861, *Official Records*, series 2, vol. 3, 148.

23. See, for example, Special Order 170, Headquarters, U.S. Army, October 12, 1861, *Official Records*, series 2, vol. 3, 51–52 (57 Confederate prisoners to be released following Confederate release of 57 U.S. prisoners).

24. Governor Sprague (R.I.) to Lincoln, October 3, 1861; Governor Andrew (Mass.) to Lincoln, November 25, 1861, both in Abraham Lincoln Papers at the Library of Congress, http://memory.loc.gov/ammem/alhtml/alhome.html; *Inside Lincoln's Cabinet*, 49 (Donald ed. 1954).

25. Joint Resolution adopted by the House of Representatives, December 11, 1861, *Official Records*, series 2, vol. 3, 157.

26. General Huger to Colonel Dimick, January 20, 1862, *Official Records,* series 2, vol. 3, 199.

27. General Wool to Adjutant General Thomas, January 24, 1861, *Official Records,* series 2, vol. 3, 212.

28. Stanton to General Wool, February 11, 1862, *Official Records,* series 2, vol. 3, 254.

29. *Official Records,* series 2, vol. 3, 302–8.

30. Stanton to General Wool, February 26, 1862, *Official Records,* series 2, vol. 3, 322.

31. General Cobb to General Wool, February 28, 1862, *Official Records,* series 2, vol. 3, 338, 339.

5. The Law as a Weapon

1. General Pope to Colonel Hurlbut, August 17, 1861, *Official Records,* series 2, vol. 1, 212.

2. Proclamation, Headquarters, Department of the West, August 30, 1861, *Official Records,* series 2, vol. 1, 221.

3. Allan Nevins, *Frémont: Pathmarker of the West,* 499–500 (1992 reprint of 1955 ed.).

4. General Frémont to Colonel Taylor, September 14, 1861, *Official Records,* series 2, vol. 1, 226.

5. See, for example, General Halleck to General Pope, December 31, 1861, series 2, vol. 1, 242.

6. Proclamation, Headquarters, Western Department, August 30, 1861, *Official Records,* series 2, vol. 1, 221.

7. See, for example, Joshua F. Speed to Lincoln, September 3, 1861, Abraham Lincoln Papers at the Library of Congress, http://memory.loc.gov/ammem/alhtml/malhome.html; telegram from Robert Anderson to Lincoln, September 13, 1861, Abraham Lincoln Papers at the Library of Congress, http://memory.loc.gov/ammem/alhtml/malhome.html. General Robert Anderson, the hero of Fort Sumter, was a native Kentuckian who had been ordered to the Midwest to rally pro-Union Kentuckians to support the administration.

8. Lincoln to General Frémont, September 11, 1861, *Collected Works,* vol. 4, 517.

9. David H. Donald, *"We Are Lincoln Men,"* 103–7 (2003).

10. Browning to Lincoln, September 17, 1861, Abraham Lincoln Papers at the Library of Congress, http://memory.loc.gov/ammem/alhtml/malhome.html, accessed July 10, 2004.

11. Lincoln to Browning, September 22, 1861, *Collected Works,* vol. 4, 531 (emphasis in original).

12. Donald, *"We Are Lincoln Men,"* 127.

13. Guelzo, *Lincoln's Emancipation Proclamation,* 52 (2004).

14. "The Heroic Age in Washington" [lecture, 1871], in *At Lincoln's Side: John Hay's Civil War Correspondence and Selected Writings,* 113, 127 (M. Burlingame ed. 2000).

15. J. G. Holland, *Life of Abraham Lincoln,* 392 (1866).

16. Annual Message to Congress, December 8, 1863, *Collected Works,* vol. 7, 36, 49.

17. Browning to Lincoln, April 30, 1861, Abraham Lincoln Papers at the Library of Congress, http://memory.loc.gov/ammem/alhtml/malhome.html, accessed July 11, 2004. Shortly after the firing on Fort Sumter on April 12, 1861, Senator Sumner advised the president that under the war power he could emancipate slaves. Donald, *Charles Sumner and the Coming of the Civil War,* 388 (1961).

18. Erastus Wright to Lincoln, September 20, 1861, Abraham Lincoln Papers at the Library of Congress, http://memory.loc.gov/ammem/alhtml/malhome.html, accessed December 7, 2004.

19. "Emancipation Our Best Weapon," October 1, 1861, in *The Works of Charles Sumner,* vol. 6, 7 (Boston, 1880).

20. Donald, *"We Are Lincoln Men,"* 106–8 (2003).

21. Browning to Lincoln, September 30, 1861, Abraham Lincoln Papers at the Library of Congress, http://memory.loc.gov/ammem/alhtml/malhome.html, accessed July 12, 2004.

22. Browning's quotations are from part IV, ch. VI, of Thomas Nugent's 1752 English translation of Burlamaqui's *Principles of Politic Law* (1748). Why Browning chose the obscure Burlamaqui [1694–1748] as his authority on the law of war is a minor mystery. In the first half of the nineteenth century, American lawyers and judges overwhelmingly relied on Emmerich de Vattel's *Law of Nations* (1758) as the principal authority on such questions. See Nussbaum, *A Concise History of the Law of Nations,* 161–63 (rev. ed. 1954). In 1861, Vattel was far more likely than Burlamaqui to be available in Quincy, Illinois.

23. See Burrus M. Carnahan, "Lincoln, Lieber and the Laws of War: The Origins and Limits of the Principle of Military Necessity," *American Journal of International Law,* vol. 92, 213 (1998).

24. See General Order 30, Headquarters, Department of the Missouri, April 22, 1863, *Official Records,* series 1, vol. 22, part 2, 237, 241–42.

25. McClellan to Buell, November 12, 1861, *Official Records,* series 2, vol. 2, 136.

26. Lincoln to General Frémont, September 2, 1861, *Collected Works,* vol. 4, 506.

27. E. J. Allen to Provost-Marshal Porter, January 13, 1862, *Official Records,* series 2, vol. 2, 1289. "E. J. Allen" was Pinkerton's pseudonym while serving as chief of intelligence for McClellan.

28. Headquarters, Army of the Potomac, to Provost-Marshal Porter, January 30, 1862, *Official Records,* series 2, vol. 2, 1292.

29. Secretary Stanton to General Halleck, April 5, 1862, *Official Records,* series 2, vol. 1, 276.

30. Adjutant General Thomas to General Frémont, April 9, 1862, *Official Records,* series 2, vol. 2, 283.

6. Congress Acts and the Confederacy Responds

1. General Butler to General Scott, May 25, 1861, *Official Records,* series 1, vol. 2, 648–51.

2. General Scott to Simon Cameron, ibid., 652.

3. Simon Cameron to General Butler, May 30, 1861, *Official Records,* series 2, vol. 1, 754–55.

4. *Harper's Weekly,* June 15, 1861, 371.

5. Simon Cameron to General Thomas, October 14, 1861, *Official Records,* series 1, vol. 6, 176–77.

6. Butler may have first publicly used the term "contraband" in a letter written from Fortress Monroe on July 30, 1861. See *The Works of Charles Sumner,* vol. 6, 32 (Boston, 1880).

7. "Act to Confiscate Property used for Insurrectionary Purposes," August 6, 1861, 12 Stat. 319.

8. Guelzo, *Lincoln's Emancipation Proclamation,* 38–41 (2004).

9. Donald, *Lincoln,* 343 (1995); *Recollected Words of Abraham Lincoln,* 64 (Fehrenbacher and Fehrenbacher eds. 1996). In April 1862, Lincoln reportedly gave such assurances to a group of delegates of freedmen's associations. Ibid., 9. The Fehrenbachers believe that there is "above average" reason to doubt this latter report.

10. Guelzo, *Lincoln's Emancipation Proclamation,* 41–42 (2004).

11. Act of August 2, 1861, 12 Stat. 285.

12. Harrison, *Lincoln of Kentucky,* 243–44 (2000).

13. General Order 12, Department of Western Virginia, February 17, 1862, *Official Records,* series 2, vol. 3, 274.

14. Journal of the Confederate Congress, vol. 1, 370 (U.S. Government Printing Office, 1905).

15. Ibid., 385, 457.

7. Military Necessity and Lincoln's Concept of the War

1. 48 U.S. (7 Howard) 1, 46 (1849) (emphasis added).

2. See "Fragment: Niagara Falls" ca. September 1848, *Collected Works,* vol. 2, 10.

3. Lincoln to General Buell, January 13, 1862, *Collected Works,* vol. 5, 98.

4. Lincoln to Charles D. Robinson (draft), August 17, 1864, *Collected Works*, vol. 7, 499, 500.

5. *Recollected Words of Abraham Lincoln*, 426 (Fehrenbacher and Fehrenbacher eds. 1996). The editors give Stoddard's statement a ranking of "D," reflecting their judgment that it is a quotation "about whose authenticity there is more than average doubt."

6. *McCulloch v. Maryland*, 4 Wheaton 316, 421 (1819).

7. "Opinion on the Constitutionality of a National Bank," February 15, 1791, in *Thomas Jefferson: Writings*, 416, 419 (Library of America, 1984).

8. *Recollected Words of Abraham Lincoln*, 469, 471 (Fehrenbacher and Fehrenbacher eds. 1996).

9. Ibid., 79, 83.

10. Phillip S. Paludan, *The Presidency of Abraham Lincoln*, 128–29 (1994).

11. Lincoln to Seward, June 28, 1862, *Collected Works*, vol. 5, 291–92.

12. See Hunter to Stanton, March 27, 1862, *Official Records*, series 1, vol. 6, 254; Hunter to Stanton, April 22, 1862, *Official Records*, series 1, vol. 14, 337; Edward A. Miller, *Lincoln's Abolitionist General*, 96–97 (1997).

13. General Order 7, Department of the South, April 13, 1862, *Official Records*, series 2, vol. 1, 815.

14. Section 1, article 58, "Act for establishing Rules and Articles for the government of the Armies of the United States," April 10, 1806, *U.S. Statutes at Large*, vol. 2, 359, 364.

15. Miller, *Lincoln's Abolitionist General*, 98 (1997).

16. War Department to General Thomas, October 14, 1861, *Official Records*, series 1, vol. 6, 176. Cameron was eventually removed as secretary of war in part because he tried to publish an official report advocating the arming of slaves. This order may have been an early reflection of his thinking on this subject.

17. General Order 11, Headquarters, Department of the South, May 9, 1862, *Official Records*, series 2, vol. 1, 818.

18. Article 40, General Order 100, War Department, Adjutant General's Office, April 24, 1863, *Official Records*, series 2, vol. 5, 671; *Miller v. United States*, 78 U.S. 267, 313 (1870); *Semmes v. United States*, 91 U.S. 21, 27 (1875).

19. *The Antelope*, 23 U.S. 66, 120 (1825).

20. Speech at Springfield, Illinois, November 4, 1854, *Collected Works*, vol. 2, 240, 245.

21. Frank Freidel, *Francis Lieber: Nineteenth-Century Liberal*, 328 (1968 reprint of 1947 edition).

22. Proclamation, May 19, 1862, *Collected Works*, vol. 5, 222.

23. Miller, *Lincoln's Abolitionist General*, 102–3 (1997).

24. Appeal to Border-State Representatives for Compensated Emancipation, July 12, 1862, *Collected Works*, vol. 5, 317–18.

25. General McClellan to Lincoln, July 7, 1862, in *The Civil War Papers of George B. McClellan,* 344–45 (Sears ed. 1989).

26. Lincoln to General Buell, January 13, 1862, *Collected Works,* vol. 5, 98.

27. *Recollected Words of Abraham Lincoln,* 469 (Fehrenbacher and Fehrenbacher eds. 1996).

28. *Inside Lincoln's Cabinet,* 95 (Donald ed. 1954)

29. Section 6, "Act to suppress Insurrection, to punish Treason and Rebellion, to seize and confiscate the Property of Rebels, and for other Purposes," July 17, 1862, 12 Stat. 589, 591.

30. Guelzo, *Lincoln's Emancipation Proclamation,* 65–66 (2004).

31. Thomas Ewing to Lincoln, June 2, 1862, Abraham Lincoln Papers at the Library of Congress, http://memory.loc.gov/ammem/alhtml/malhome. html.

32. See *Miller v. United States,* 78 U.S. 267, 313 (1870); *Semmes v. United States,* 91 U.S. 21, 27 (1875).

33. 54 U.S. at 134.

34. Lincoln to Cuthbert Bullitt, July 28, 1862, *Collected Works,* vol. 5, 344–45.

35. General Halleck to General Saxton, August 25, 1862, *Official Records,* series 1, vol. 14, 377–78.

36. Lincoln to Chase, September 2, 1863, *Collected Works,* vol. 6, 428–29.

37. Lincoln to General Reynolds, January 20, 1865, *Collected Works,* vol. 8, 228–29.

38. Randall, *Constitutional Problems under Lincoln,* 359 (rev. ed. 1951).

39. "Order Concerning the Confiscation Act," November 13, 1862, *Collected Works,* vol. 5, 496.

40. General Schofield to Secretary of War Stanton, July 17, 1863, *Official Records,* series 3, vol. 3, 525; Judge Advocate General Holt to Stanton, *Official Records,* series 2, vol. 6, 209–10. See also Randall, *Constitutional Problems under Lincoln,* 361 (rev. ed. 1951).

41. See Special Order 288, Department of the Gulf, August 22, 1862, *Official Records,* series 2, vol. 4, 418: "Edward Le Beau having in conjunction with Edgar Le Beau against the orders of the commanding general of this department destroyed arms belonging to the Confederate States for the purpose of depriving the United States of the use of the arms and having buried arms for the purpose of depriving the United States of them, are sentenced to confinement on Ship Island for the term of one year. The arms will be confiscated, and the negro boy who gave the information of the concealed arms—George Washington Walker—will be emancipated. The proper act of emancipation will be made out by the provost court for that purpose."

42. See "James C. Welling," in *Reminiscences of Abraham Lincoln by Distinguished Men of His Time,* 547–48 (1971 reprint of 1888 ed.); Randall, *Constitu-*

tional Problems under Lincoln, 383–84 (rev. ed. 1951) (quoting Richard Henry Dana, "one of the ablest lawyers of that day").

43. See Freidel, *Francis Lieber*, 318–19 (1968 reprint of 1947 ed.); Harold M. Hyman, *A More Perfect Union: The Impact of Civil War and Reconstruction on the Constitution*, 192–93 (Sentry edition, 1975).

44. "Rights of Sovereignty and Rights of War," speech delivered May 9, 1862, in *The Works of Charles Sumner*, vol. 7, 9, 44 (Boston, 1874).

45. Vattel, *Law of Nations*, book III, section 203 (J. Chitty trans. 1852).

46. Salmon P. Chase to Lincoln, December 31, 1862, Abraham Lincoln Papers at the Library of Congress, http://memory.loc.gov/ammem/alhtml/malhome.html; Charles Sumner to George Livermore, January 6, 1863, in *The Selected Letters of Charles Sumner*, vol. 2, 139–40 (Palmer ed. 1990).

8. The Proclamation as a Weapon of War

1. "Act to make an additional Article of War," March 13, 1862, 12 Stat. 354. On July 9, 1861, the House of Representatives had adopted a resolution that ". . . in the judgment of this House it is no part of the duty of the soldiers of the United States to capture and return fugitives." *Official Records*, series 2, vol. 1, 759. In December, Congressman Owen Lovejoy, an Illinois abolitionist, introduced legislation to turn this nonbinding resolution into law by amending the Articles of War. Guelzo, *Lincoln's Emancipation Proclamation*, 64 (2004).

2. General Butler to General Phelps, May 23, 1862, *Official Records*, series 1, vol. 15, 443.

3. Major Peck to General Phelps, Camp Parapet, La., June 16, 1862, *Official Records*, series 1, vol. 15, 491.

4. General Phelps to Captain Davis (Butler's adjutant), June 16, 1862, *Official Records*, series 1, vol. 15, 486–90.

5. Secretary Stanton to General Butler, June 29, 1862, *Official Records*, series 1, vol. 15, 515–16.

6. Lincoln to Reverdy Johnson, July 26, 1862, *Collected Works*, vol. 5, 342–43.

7. "Reply to Emancipation Memorial Presented by Chicago Christians of All Denominations," *Collected Works*, vol. 5, 419–25.

8. See Guelzo, *Lincoln's Emancipation Proclamation*, 180 (2004). *Cf.* George Anastaplo, *Abraham Lincoln: A Constitutional Biography*, 219–20 (1999).

9. Emancipation Proclamation, January 1, 1863, *Collected Works*, vol. 6, 28–30.

10. See *Inside Lincoln's Cabinet*, 99–100 (Donald ed. 1954); Guelzo, *Lincoln's Emancipation Proclamation*, 187 (2004).

11. General Hunter to Secretary Stanton, July 11, 1862, *Official Records*, series 1, vol. 14, 363.

12. Paludan, *The Presidency of Abraham Lincoln*, 146 (1994).

13. General Hunter to Secretary Stanton, August 4, 1862, *Official Records,* series 3, vol. 2, 292.

14. General Hunter to Secretary Stanton, August 10, 1862, *Official Records,* series 3, vol. 2, 346.

15. General Butler to Secretary Stanton, August 2, 1862, *Official Records,* series 1, vol. 15, 534. After recruiting black troops had been officially approved, the government offered Phelps a major general's commission to command them, but he refused the offer. "Phelps, John Walcott," in *The Twentieth Century Biographical Dictionary of Notable Americans,* vol. 8, n.p. (R. Johnson and J. H. Brown eds. 1904).

16. General Halleck to General Saxton, August 25, 1862, *Official Records,* series 1, vol. 14, 377–78.

17. Lincoln to Johnson, March 27, 1863, *Collected Works,* vol. 6, 149–50.

18. Lincoln to Hunter, April 1, 1863, *Collected Works,* vol. 6, 158.

19. Annual Message to Congress, December 8, 1863, *Collected Works,* vol. 7, 36, 51; Proclamation of Amnesty and Reconstruction, December 8, 1863, *Collected Works,* vol. 7, 53, 54; Annual Message to Congress, December 6, 1864, *Collected Works,* vol. 8, 136, 152.

20. Lincoln to Charles D. Robinson, August 17, 1864, *Collected Works,* vol. 7, 499–501.

21. Memorandum on Probable Failure of Re-Election, August 23, 1864, *Collected Works,* vol. 7, 514.

22. General Order 111, Confederate States Army, December 23, 1862, *Official Records,* series 1, vol. 15, 906.

23. Howard Jones, "History and Mythology: The Crisis over British Intervention in the Civil War," in *The Union, the Confederacy and the Atlantic Rim,* 29, 43–45 (R. May ed. 1995).

24. See Salmon P. Chase to Lincoln, December 31, 1862 (Recommended alterations to the Emancipation Proclamation) and Final Emancipation Proclamation—Preliminary Draft, with suggested changes by William H. Seward, [December 30, 1862], both in Abraham Lincoln Papers at the Library of Congress, http://memory.loc.gov/ammem/alhtml/malhome.html.

25. Freidel, *Francis Lieber,* 318 (1968 reprint of 1947 ed.).

26. Ibid., 328.

27. "Instructions for the Government of Armies of the United States in the Field," April 24, 1863, in *The Laws of Armed Conflicts,* 3, 11 (D. Schindler and J. Toman eds. 1981).

28. See General Hitchcock to Secretary Stanton, April 29, 1863, *Official Records,* series 2, vol. 5, 470; Ware to Brown, April 8, 1863, ibid., 455. Brown and Ware were the military secretary to the governor of Massachusetts and the assistant military secretary, respectively. Hitchcock had personal reasons for distrusting the Confederate leadership, having resigned from the army in 1855

as a result of a dispute with Secretary of War Jefferson Davis. John C. Fredriksen, *American Military Leaders*, vol. 1, 340–41 (1995).

29. See, for example, the July 1863 correspondence between generals Halleck and Ludlow on the reported hanging of captured black soldiers, *Official Records*, series 2, vol 6, 73, 289; on August 2, 1863, Secretary Stanton telegraphed the governor of Massachusetts for any further evidence he might have of abuse of Massachusetts black soldiers; none was found. Ibid., 189.

30. Charles Sumner to Lincoln, May 20, 1863, Abraham Lincoln Papers at the Library of Congress, http://memory.loc.gov/ammem/alhtml/malhome.html.

31. Order of Retaliation, July 30, 1863, *Collected Works*, vol. 6, 357; *Official Records*, series 2, vol. 6, 163.

32. "The persons excepted from the benefits of the foregoing provisions are . . . all who have engaged in any way in treating colored persons, or white persons in charge of such, otherwise than lawfully as prisoners of war. . . ." Proclamation of Amnesty and Reconstruction, December 8, 1863, *Official Records*, series 2, vol. 6, 681.

33. The text of this order has been lost, but the 1863 annual report of the commissary for exchange to the secretary of war stated that "an order was sent by the President to our commanders in the field not to grant paroles, and to make no exchanges, without orders from the War Department." Hitchcock to Stanton, November 30, 1863, *Official Records*, series 2, vol. 6, 607–14. This order was probably issued sometime after August 25, 1863, when the Confederate exchange commissioner finally ceased evading the issue and unequivocally told General Hitchcock that the CSA would never recognize former slaves as prisoners of war. See ibid., 226.

34. Article 16, Convention Relative to the Treatment of Prisoners of War, August 12, 1849, 6 U.S.T. 3316, T.I.A.S. No. 3364.

9. The Conkling Letter

1. See Guelzo, *Lincoln's Emancipation Proclamation*, 186–202 (2004).

2. 67 U.S. 635 (1863).

3. See Ronald C. White, *The Eloquent President*, 197 (2005).

4. Conkling to Lincoln, August 14, 1863, Abraham Lincoln Papers at the Library of Congress, http://memory.loc.gov/ammem/alhtml/alhome.html, accessed July 12, 2004.

5. White, *The Eloquent President*, 195 (2005).

6. See Donald, *Lincoln*, 457–58 (1995); Harry J. Maihafer, *War of Words*, 131–32 (2001).

7. Lincoln to Conkling, August 26, 1863, *Collected Works*, vol. 6, 406.

8. Burlamaqui, *Principles of Politic Law*, 281–82 (The Lawbook Exchange, Ltd. 2003 facsimile reprint of the 1752 edition of Nugent's translation).

9. Address at Cooper Institute, New York City, February 27, 1860, *Collected Works*, vol. 3, 522, 537.

10. A Radical Recognition of Freedom

1. "The Emancipation Moment: Lincoln's Other 'First of January,'" *Lincoln Lore* no. 1880, 2 (spring 2005).

2. See Guelzo, "How Abe Lincoln Lost the Black Vote," *Journal of the Abraham Lincoln Association*, vol. 25, no. 1, 1–22 (winter 2004); Kevin Fields, "Historiographical Trends and Interpretations of President Abraham Lincoln's Reputation and Morality on the Slavery Question," part 1 in the *Lincoln Herald*, vol. 106, 150 (winter 2004), part 2 in vol. 107, 11 (spring 2005).

3. Definition of Aggression, United Nations General Assembly Resolution 3314 (XXIX) (December 14, 1974), Annex, article 5, paragraph 3.

Index